# Improving Mathematics and Science Education

A Longitudinal Investigation of the Relationship Between Reform-Oriented Instruction and Student Achievement

Vi-Nhuan Le, Brian M. Stecher, J. R. Lockwood, Laura S. Hamilton, Abby Robyn, Valerie L. Williams, Gery Ryan, Kerri A. Kerr, José Felipe Martínez, Stephen P. Klein

Sponsored by the National Science Foundation

RAND EDUCATION

The research described in this report was sponsored by the National Science Foundation and was conducted by RAND Education, a unit of the RAND Corporation.

**Library of Congress Cataloging-in-Publication Data**

Improving mathematics and science education : a longitudinal investigation of the relationship between reform-oriented instruction and student achievement / Vi-Nhuan Le ... [et al.].
    p. cm.
Includes bibliographical references.
ISBN-13: 978-0-8330-3964-4 (pbk. : alk. paper)
    1. Mathematics—Study and teaching (Elementary)—United States. 2. Science—Study and teaching (Elementary)—United States. 3. Education—Aims and objectives—United States. 4. Academic achievement—United States.
I. Le, Vi-Nhuan.

QA135.6.I47 2006
372.7—dc22

2006016941

The RAND Corporation is a nonprofit research organization providing objective analysis and effective solutions that address the challenges facing the public and private sectors around the world. RAND's publications do not necessarily reflect the opinions of its research clients and sponsors.

RAND® is a registered trademark.

Published 2006 by the RAND Corporation
1776 Main Street, P.O. Box 2138, Santa Monica, CA 90407-2138
1200 South Hayes Street, Arlington, VA 22202-5050
4570 Fifth Avenue, Suite 600, Pittsburgh, PA 15213-2665
RAND URL: http://www.rand.org/
To order RAND documents or to obtain additional information, contact Distribution Services: Telephone: (310) 451-7002;
Fax: (310) 451-6915; Email: order@rand.org

# Preface

The term *reform-oriented teaching* describes a collection of instructional practices that are designed to engage students as active participants in their own learning and to enhance the development of complex cognitive skills and processes. This monograph presents the results of a multiyear, National Science Foundation (NSF)-funded study of the effect of reform-oriented mathematics and science teaching on student achievement.

The research was conducted in three districts that participated in the NSF Local Systemic Change program, although the study is not an evaluation of the implementation or impact of that specific program. By following students for three years and by using innovative measures of practice, this study extends prior RAND research on mathematics and science instructional practices:

- S. Klein, L. Hamilton, D. McCaffrey, B. Stecher, A. Robyn, and D. Burroughs, *Teaching Practices and Student Achievement: Report of First-Year Findings from the "Mosaic" Study of Systematic Initiatives in Mathematics and Science*, MR-1233-EDU, 2000.
- L. Hamilton, D. McCaffrey, B. Stecher, S. Klein, A. Robyn, and D. Bugliari, "Studying Large-Scale Reforms of Instructional Practice: An Example from Mathematics and Science," *Educational Evaluation and Policy Analysis*, Vol. 25, No. 1, 2003, pp. 1–29.

Results should be of interest to educators and policymakers concerned with improving mathematics and science education. Appendixes supporting the results and providing background information are included on the CD-ROM inside the back cover.

The study was carried out by RAND Education, a unit of the RAND Corporation, and was sponsored by NSF. It is part of a larger body of RAND Education work addressing teachers and teaching, mathematics and science achievement, and instructional reforms.

# Contents

# Figures

# Tables

# Summary

## Background and Purpose

*Reform-oriented teaching* is a collection of instructional practices that was a prominent feature of reforms in mathematics and science education beginning in the 1990s. Such practices, which are consistent with the National Science Education Standards (National Research Council, 1996), stressed instruction that engages students as active participants in their own learning and emphasizes the development of complex cognitive skills and processes. Despite large investments in the promotion of reform-oriented curricula and instruction, the evidence supporting the effectiveness of these practices in raising mathematics and science achievement is relatively weak.

This monograph presents the findings of a multiyear study of the effectiveness of reform-oriented mathematics and science instruction. It builds on an earlier RAND study, called the Mosaic project, which found "a weak but positive relationship" between reform practices and student achievement (see Klein, Hamilton, McCaffrey, Stecher, Robyn, and Burroughs, 2000; Hamilton, McCaffrey, Stecher, Klein, Robyn, and Bugliari, 2003). The present study, called Mosaic II, extends this earlier research in two important ways. First, it incorporates more-diverse indicators of student exposure to reform-oriented practices, including innovative, vignette-based measures. Second, it follows students for three years to measure the relationship after longer exposure. Similar to the earlier research, this study uses multiple measures of achievement, including open-ended assessments, to determine whether the relationship is sensitive to the manner in which achievement is measured.

Mosaic II was designed to answer two major research questions:

- Is the use of reform-oriented instructional practices in mathematics and science associated with higher student achievement?
- Is the relationship between reform-oriented practices and achievement sensitive to the aspects of achievement that are measured?

## Methods

Mosaic II is an observational study, relying on naturally occurring variation in teaching practices as the basis for uncovering relationships between reform-oriented practice and student outcomes. That is, the design assumes that there is substantial variation in teaching practices among teachers within a school, even though teachers may have been exposed to the same training. To find a sample of teachers that encompassed a range of different instructional approaches, including reform-oriented instruction, we selected three districts that had recently concluded their participation in the Local Systemic Change program, a five-year National Science Foundation initiative to promote reform-oriented, systemic reform of mathematics and science education. Within these three districts, we selected five cohorts of students and followed each for three years beginning in the 2001–2002 school year. The cohorts varied in student age and academic subject being studied, with mathematics examined in three cohorts (grades 3 through 5; 6 through 8; and 7 through 9) and science examined in the remaining two cohorts (grades 3 through 5 and 6 through 8). All the teachers who were responsible for teaching the targeted subject (mathematics or science) to students in the five cohorts were included in the research in the year or years they taught the subject to the students.

For all five cohorts, achievement was measured using the mathematics or science component of the Stanford Achievement Test Series, Ninth Edition (SAT-9), published by Harcourt Assessment. For most analyses, only the total score was available. However, for one mathematics cohort, we also obtained the Problem-Solving and Mathematical Procedures subscale scores. In addition, in two science cohorts and one mathematics cohort, we administered the open-ended version of the SAT-9 so that we could compare students' performance on open-ended and multiple-choice measures.

A key feature of the Mosaic II study is the use of multiple measures to determine the extent to which reform-oriented teaching practices were being used in the classroom. Each year, all participating teachers completed a survey, filled out classroom logs, and responded to a set of vignette-based questions about instructional practices. In selected years, we supplemented the main data-collection procedures with classroom observations and interviews conducted with a smaller subset of teachers. We used teacher responses to the surveys, logs, and vignettes, and observers' ratings of classrooms to derive a number of measures of instructional practices, teacher background, curriculum coverage, and classroom context.

One of the innovative features of this study is the use of vignette-based measures of instructional practice. *Vignettes* are contextualized descriptions of hypothetical classroom situations that can be used to elicit information about potential teaching behaviors. In this study, vignette-based items were used to try to ascertain teachers' tendencies to use reform-oriented instructional practices. We developed two vignettes for each subject-grade combination. Each vignette contained four instructional problems that provided teachers with hypothetical classroom events at different points within the given mathematics or science unit.

After each instructional problem, teachers were presented with a list of options that reflected a range of teaching actions, from behaviors that were not associated with reform pedagogy to teacher behaviors that were consistent with reform-oriented teaching. Teachers were asked to rate their likelihood of engaging in each option, using a four-point scale from "very unlikely" to "very likely," or, for questions of emphasis, from "no emphasis" to "great emphasis."

We derived two measures from the vignettes. The first measure, Reform-High, reflects teachers' answers to the subset of high-reform response options across the two vignettes. The second measure, Reform-Full, reflects the "location" of each teacher between an "ideal" high-reform teacher and an "ideal" nonreform teacher. The ideal high-reform teacher was a simulated teacher whose self-reported likelihood of engaging in each option corresponded exactly to our judgments of reform orientation. Conversely, the ideal nonreform teacher was a simulated teacher whose self-reported likelihood was just the opposite. Analyses of the pattern of responses to these and other measures, as well as cognitive interviews conducted with a subset of teachers who described their thought processes as they answered the vignettes, suggest that the measures are providing some validity evidence about the likely use of reform-oriented instruction. The cognitive interviews also provided insights to inform potential improvements to the vignettes.

We used a multivariate linear mixed model to represent the relationship between longitudinal exposure to teacher-level predictors and student-achievement trajectories. For each outcome in each cohort, we jointly modeled test scores from the three years of the study. Scores were expressed as a linear function of overall means, adjustments for student-background variables and prior performance, current and past exposure to teacher-level predictors, unobserved random teacher effects, and residual errors that were allowed to be correlated across time within (i.e., for each) student.

We estimated the effects of teacher-level variables, including instructional practices, one at a time. That is, we started with a baseline model that includes adjustments for student demographics and year 0 (the year before the study began) achievement, and then examined the effects of a given individual teacher-level variable by augmenting the baseline model with only that particular teacher-level variable.

We report inferences about two functions of the model parameters that quantify the effects of exposure to teacher-level variables on student achievement. The first function captures the average effect of current-year exposure on current-year outcomes. The other function is the three-year cumulative exposure effect, which is interpreted as the expected difference in the scores between two students, one of whom received above-average exposure to the particular teacher-level variable under consideration for three consecutive years, and the other one of whom received average exposure for three consecutive years.

## Study Limitations

Although this study represents a methodological advance in comparison with earlier studies, it still has limitations. Stronger conclusions would have been possible using an experimental design rather than relying on naturally occurring variation. In particular, we had no control of the assignment of students to teachers during the three years of the research, and, as a result, relatively few students received either the most intensive or the least intensive exposure to reform-oriented instruction. Tracking of students in the middle schools may have confounded achievement with exposure in ways we were unable to disentangle. More-extensive use of classroom observations might provide a more accurate indication of teaching practices than do the self-report measures that were the primary tool in this study. Our experience using the vignette-based measures revealed ways these vignette-based measures might be improved in the future, as well.

## Relationships Between Reform-Oriented Instruction and Student Achievement

The first research question concerned the relationships between exposure to reform practices and student achievement. We found that exposure to reform-oriented instruction generally had nonsignificant or weak positive relationships to student achievement in both mathematics and science, with the exception of groupwork-related practices in mathematics (for which the relationships were negative). Additionally, the findings suggest that relationships tend to become stronger with sustained exposure to reform teaching.

The second research question asked whether the relationship was affected by the way achievement was measured. We generally found stronger relationships for open-ended measures than for multiple-choice measures in the sites at which both types of assessment were administered. Moreover, in the cohort with data on subscales of the multiple-choice mathematics achievement test, we found positively signed relationships to the Problem-Solving subscale and negatively signed relationships to the Procedures subscale. Together, these findings suggest that relationships between instruction and achievement can depend on how achievement is measured.

## Implications

We found nonsignificant or weak positive relationships between reform-oriented instruction in mathematics and science and student achievement measured using multiple-choice tests. The relationships were somewhat stronger when achievement was measured with open-ended assessment. Additionally, in mathematics, relationships tended to be positively signed with problem-solving scores.

These findings confirm previous estimates of weak positive associations between reform-oriented instruction and achievement. The results also reinforce the message that measurement matters—i.e., that the observed relationship between reform-oriented instruction and achievement may depend on how achievement is measured. It is common practice to use existing state or district tests as measures of program effectiveness, because it is often not feasible to administer additional tests. Our analysis indicates that this decision may influence findings. It also suggests that using subscales from an existing test to produce a more refined analysis of relationships between instruction and achievement might be a good practice.

It is also important to note the influence of high-stakes accountability testing on teaching practices. Teachers reported that the testing environment influenced their use of reform-oriented practices despite the training they had received. In particular, many teachers believed that the reform-oriented practices were likely to be less effective than other kinds of practices for promoting high scores on state accountability tests. Future research on the effectiveness of reform-oriented instruction needs to recognize that instructional reforms are not carried out in a vacuum, and it should examine the broader contextual factors as well as the specific elements of the intervention.

Perhaps the most important unanswered question regarding reform-oriented instruction concerns benefits and costs. The mathematics and science initiatives of the 1990s were relatively expensive (from the perspective of national reforms). And, although they appear to have had some effects on mathematics and science teaching, this study did not address whether these changes in practice and the associated improvements in achievement were worth the cost. Thus, it is impossible to know whether the strategy was an efficient one and should be followed in future reforms. A program of research that involves experimental studies with clear delineation of costs would provide a strong foundation for future decisions about educational reforms.

# Acknowledgments

We are indebted to the many individuals who supported us throughout this project. We are grateful to Ken Jeddeloh, Carolyn O'Reilly, and James Myerberg, whose assistance ensured successful coordination with the schools. We also appreciate the time and insights of the thousands of students and the hundreds of principals and teachers who participated in the study.

Our research would not have been possible without input from our advisory panels. We would like to acknowledge Hilda Borko, Maurene Flory, Megan Franke, James Middleton, Jody Priselac, Brian Foley, Maria Lopez-Freeman, Jerome Pine, Kathy Roth, Vandana Thadani, and Iris Weiss.

Special thanks go to Miriam Sherin, who served both as an advisory panelist and as our reviewer. Her thoughtful comments and suggestions on earlier drafts of the monograph greatly improved the final product. We would also like to thank Alicia Alonzo for her help in developing the vignettes.

A number of RAND colleagues supported us at various stages of this project. We were fortunate to have the programming skills of Delia Bugliari and the logistical help of Peter Scott. Derrick Chau proved invaluable with the vignette development and teacher interviews. Donna White, Sharon Koga, and Natalie Swenson provided much-needed assistance throughout the project. The quality of this monograph also benefited from the careful reading of Richard Buddin and Cathy Stasz, both of whom provided incisive comments on earlier versions.

Finally, special thanks go to Janice Earle for her help and encouragement, and to the National Science Foundation for its support of this project.

# Abbreviations

| | |
|---|---|
| AAAS | American Association for the Advancement of Science |
| FOSS | Full Option Science System |
| FRL | free or reduced-price lunches |
| HLM | hierarchical linear modeling |
| LSC | Local Systemic Change |
| MC | multiple choice |
| NAEP | National Assessment of Educational Progress |
| NCTM | National Council of Teachers of Mathematics |
| NRC | National Research Council |
| NSF | National Science Foundation |
| OE | open ended |
| PR | procedures |
| PS | problem solving |

SAT-9            Stanford Achievement Test Series, Ninth
                 Edition

STC             Science and Technology for Children

# CHAPTER ONE

# Introduction

## Background: Reform-Oriented Instruction in Mathematics and Science

Educators and policymakers have been concerned about the quality of mathematics and science education in the United States for several decades. In the 1990s, a number of major initiatives were launched to improve mathematics and science education, including the development of national standards (National Council of Teachers of Mathematics [NCTM], 1989, 2000; National Research Council [NRC], 1996; American Association for the Advancement of Science [AAAS], 1993); the development of new curriculum materials (Linn et al., 2000; Porter et al., 1994); the initiation of systemic reforms (Shields, Corcoran, and Zucker, 1994); the provision of professional development (Dutro et al., 2002); and the development of new assessment strategies (Stecher and Klein, 1996).

One prominent feature in these efforts was a new approach to teaching mathematics and science, referred to as "reform-oriented teaching." This approach stressed instruction that engages students as active participants in their own learning and that seeks to enhance the development of complex cognitive skills and processes. Students are asked to "do mathematics" and "do science" in ways that are similar to those engaged in by mathematicians and scientists. Prominent organizations embraced this approach, including NCTM, NRC, and AAAS. Reform-oriented approaches were adopted in many schools and districts across the country, although even at their most popular they were less frequently used than were more traditional approaches (Desimone et al., 2005; Ravitz, Becker, and Wong, 2000).

Despite the great investments in the promotion of reform-oriented teaching, the evidence supporting the effectiveness of its practices in mathematics and science is relatively weak. Studies that have examined the relationship between student achievement and teacher reports of reform-based instruction suggest that these practices may contribute to student achievement, but in most cases the effects appear to be quite small. Wenglinsky (2002) reported moderate relationships between a set of reform-based practices and student mathematics achievement on the National Assessment of Educational Progress (NAEP). Using data from the *High School Effectiveness Study, 1990–1992* from the National Longitudinal Study of 1988 (U.S. Department of Education, 1997), Von Secker and Lissitz (1999) found that students' reported exposure to reform-oriented pedagogy was associated with higher science achievement, although the relationships were statistically modest. Similar results are described in studies by Smith, Lee, and Newmann (2001) in mathematics and by Smerdon, Burkam, and Lee (1999) in science. Synthesizing data from 11 National Science Foundation (NSF)-funded sites that were promoting reform instruction, Hamilton et al. (2003) found a mixture of nonsignificant and small positive results. These findings are similar to those obtained by Mayer (1998); using regression analyses, Mayer observed weak positive or nonsignificant relationships between reform-based practices and student scores on a standardized mathematics multiple-choice test.

Of particular interest is whether reform-oriented teaching can enhance scientific or mathematical communication, problem solving, or other higher-order thinking skills. Many advocates of reform teaching believe that traditional multiple-choice tests do not adequately reflect these types of competencies, and that alternative tests that require students to construct their own responses or engage in problem solving are more likely to detect changes in these competencies and, hence, the effect of reform-oriented teaching.

There is some evidence of a positive, albeit weak, relationship between reform instruction and higher-order thinking measured using open-ended responses. A study by Cohen and Hill (2000) revealed an association between reform-oriented instruction and higher scores on the California Learning Assessment System mathematics test, a performance-based assessment designed to measure students' understanding of mathematics problems and procedures. Thompson and Senk (2001) found that reform-oriented practices that emphasized explanations of how problems were solved, in conjunction with a reform-oriented curriculum, correlated positively with mathematics achievement, especially on multistep problems and problems involving applications or graphical representations in mathematics. Similarly, Saxe, Gearhart, and Seltzer (1999) found that reform-oriented instruction was associated with students' performance on mathematics problem solving, but not with their performance on factual knowledge or computation. Finally, Hamilton et al. (2003) reported stronger effects of reform teaching on open-ended tests than on multiple-choice assessments. However, few of these studies directly compared the effects of reform teaching on problem-solving skills relative to procedural skills or provided effect-size estimates that could be directly compared with those reported above.

## Focus of the Mosaic II Study

This monograph presents the findings of a multiyear study of the effectiveness of reform-oriented mathematics and science instruction. This is the second research project undertaken by RAND to examine the effectiveness of reform-oriented instruction. It builds on an earlier study that used multiple achievement measures from 11 sites to assemble a "mosaic" of evidence regarding the relationships between mathematics and science achievement and reform-oriented practices (see Klein et al., 2000; Hamilton et al., 2003). The Mosaic study found "a weak but positive relationship" between reform practices and student achievement, one that was "somewhat stronger" when achievement was measured with open-response tests than with multiple-choice tests.

## Mosaic II Study Design

The present study, called Mosaic II, was conducted in districts that were participating in the NSF's Local Systemic Change (LSC) program, a large-scale, national initiative to improve mathematics and science instruction and achievement.[1] The program, started in 1995, has funded nearly 90 projects across the country, and fosters systemic reform, in which standards, curriculum materials, assessments, teacher preparation, and other parts of the educational system are aligned to guide instruction and student learning (Webb, 1997; Smith and O'Day, 1991). LSC initiatives, in particular, focus on professional development to increase teachers' use of reform-oriented instruction.[2]

The systemic approach adopted in LSC programs was designed to address shortcomings in previous piecemeal reform efforts that sent inconsistent signals to teachers (e.g., implementing a new curriculum but retaining the old assessments, or training teachers to use new instructional methods but retaining the old textbooks). By coordinating all aspects of the system, LSC districts hoped to send clear and consistent signals to teachers reinforcing effective practices. However, the program did not have an explicit theory of learning that posited how each of the elements was related to student achievement or how the elements were interrelated.

Mosaic II strengthens the former Mosaic study in two important ways. First, it broadens the measures of teaching practices to include multiple indicators of instruction, including innovative vignette-based measures and teacher logs, to obtain more-sensitive indicators of student exposure to reform-oriented practices. Second, it follows students for three years to measure the relationship after longer exposure. These

---

[1] Note that the study is not an evaluation of the LSC program, but of the underlying relationship between specific instructional practices and student achievement. The extent to which these many LSC components are coordinated and work in concert to promote achievement has been the focus of other studies (Borman and Kersaint, 2002; Corcoran, Shields, and Zucker, 1998; Shields, Marsh, and Adelman, 1998; Russon, Stark, and Horn, 2000).

[2] According to http://lsc-net.terc.edu/go.cfm, a Web site that serves to facilitate sharing of best practices among LSC projects, all projects require long-term professional development of at least 100 hours for teachers at targeted grades, with a focus on disciplinary knowledge and pedagogical skills.

improvements were intended to provide greater sensitivity to various instructional practices and a better opportunity to examine cumulative relationships between reform-oriented instructional practices and student achievement. As does its predecessor, Mosaic II uses multiple measures of achievement to test whether the relationship between instructional practices and achievement is sensitive to the manner in which achievement is measured.

**Expanded Measures of Instructional Practice**
One key feature of this study is the use of more-extensive and more-varied measures of instructional practice, including teacher logs and vignette-based measures. The weak relationships found in the first Mosaic study may have stemmed, in part, from the exclusive use of frequency-based survey items to measure reform-oriented instruction. While these types of surveys have proven to be a cost-effective method for collecting general descriptions of classroom events, they also have limitations (Kennedy, 1999). Surveys, for example, cannot capture subtleties in how teachers understand terminology used to describe instruction (Burstein et al., 1995; Cohen, 1990; Mayer, 1999; Spillane and Zeuli, 1999; Stigler and Perry, 2000). For instance, the mathematics reform community uses the term *problem solving* to indicate the processes that students engage in when they work on novel problems with no immediate solution (Schoenfeld, 1989). Teachers, however, tend to use the term to represent more-traditional practices, such as solving word problems with fairly straightforward solutions (Hill, 2005).

The shortcomings of surveys have led to calls for better methods to measure instructional practices (Henke, Chen, and Goldman, 1999; Hoachlander, Griffith, and Ralph, 1996). The use of vignettes is one alternative. Vignettes are contextualized descriptions of hypothetical classroom situations that can be used to elicit information about potential teaching behaviors. In this study, vignette-based items were used to try to ascertain teachers' tendencies to use reform-oriented instructional practices. Vignette-based items can make data collection more realistic by providing teachers with a classroom context in which to situate their responses (Kennedy, 1999). In addition, although vignettes contain valuable contextual details, they are standardized; therefore, responses from teachers can be aggregated and compared (Kennedy, 1999; Ma, 1999; Ruiz-Primo and Li, 2002).

Vignettes also have limitations as indicators of classroom instruction. They impose a greater reading burden on teachers than do traditional surveys, and the resources needed to generate the hypothetical classroom situations may render vignettes more costly to develop. Because vignettes have had limited use, there is scant evidence about their validity as measures of teaching practices. Research in psychology has found that expressed intentions are a good predictor of future behavior (Ajzen and Fishbein, 1980), which suggests that responses to vignettes might reflect actual teaching practices. Indeed, Ruiz-Primo and Li (2002) found that the quality of teacher feedback provided on hypothetical journal entries corresponded to teachers' feedback on their students' science notebooks from a previous year. Classroom vignettes hold promise as measures of teaching practice, and their use in this study may strengthen our findings while also providing additional evidence about their validity.

### Longitudinal Data and Analysis

A second key feature of this study is its longitudinal design. To date, research on instructional interventions has involved cross-sectional designs that compare the achievement of treated and untreated students after one year of exposure. This study was designed to follow cohorts of students and measure their exposure to reform-oriented instruction over three years. In most cases, we have an initial measure of achievement collected in the spring of the year before the study, followed by annual measures of achievement and exposure collected in the spring of the subsequent three years. By increasing the length of the exposure, we hope to increase its "signal" and, hence, our ability to detect it from the "noise" of background factors and other classroom influences.

### Multiple Outcome Measures

Finally, the study uses multiple outcome measures to broaden the domains of mathematics and science achievement that are considered. As noted above, research suggests that reform-oriented practice may improve achievement in some aspects of mathematics and science more than in others. In particular, scientific and mathematical communication, problem solving, and other higher-order thinking skills may be enhanced by reform-oriented instruction more than are basic factual knowledge and structured procedural skills. This study uses both multiple-choice and open-ended measures to examine the effect of reform-oriented instruction on both types of outcomes. In science, we used both the multiple-choice and the open-ended versions of the Stanford Achievement Test Series, Ninth Edition (SAT-9) test; the open-ended version is designed to measure scientific inquiry, decision-making and problem solving, and conceptual understanding (Harcourt Assessment, 1996a). In mathematics, all students completed the SAT-9 multiple-choice test, and one cohort also completed the SAT-9 open-ended tasks, which require students to show the reasoning behind their answers (Harcourt Assessment, 1996b). In addition, we used two sub-scales from the SAT-9 multiple-choice test in one cohort to differentiate procedural knowledge of mathematics from mathematical problem solving.

## Research Questions

To recapitulate, the study was designed to answer two major research questions:

- Is the use of reform-oriented instructional practices in mathematics and science associated with higher student achievement?
- Is the relationship between reform-oriented practices and achievement sensitive to the aspects of achievement that are measured?

## Importance of the Study

The problem of fostering effective mathematics and science education continues to vex the nation, and the findings of this study will help educators in their quest for effective instructional methods. A recent report from the National Academies raised a number of red flags about the performance of U.S. students. For example, U.S. twelfth-graders performed below the international average for 21 countries on a test of mathematics and science achievement. Although the performance of American fourth- and eighth-graders exceeded the international average in both subjects (Mullis et al., 2004), U.S. students' scores lagged behind those of a number of other countries and did not increase as quickly as the scores of those of some other nations. In 2005, a congressionally convened panel of business and education leaders warned that the United States was losing its leadership in mathematics and science. The panel concluded that the economic future of the United States depends on its ability to improve K–12 mathematics and science education (Committee on Science, Engineering, and Public Policy, 2006). In this context, it is essential to know whether reform-oriented teaching holds the key toward better mathematics and science education.

## Organization of This Monograph

Chapter Two of this monograph describes the research procedures, including samples, participation rates, measures, and methods of analysis. Chapter Three discusses the development and the technical quality of the instructional-practice measures. Chapter Four presents the findings, highlighting the relationships between reform-oriented teaching and student mathematics and science achievement. Chapter Five summarizes the findings and discusses implications of the results for practice and policy.

# CHAPTER TWO

# Sample Selection and Data Collection

The study followed five cohorts of students and their mathematics and science teachers over a three-year period. This chapter provides details about the methods that were used to select sites and to sample schools, teachers, and students. It also describes data-collection procedures, including the surveys, logs, interviews, and observations that were used to assess information about teachers' background characteristics, instructional practices, and classroom influences.

## Site, School, and Grade-Level Selection

The project recruited school districts that had participated or were participating in NSF's LSC program. NSF staff familiar with the LSC program suggested districts they believed had high teacher participation in reform-oriented professional development, and we solicited participation from these districts. Participation in the study required the administration of additional achievement tests other than the state test to students and instructional-practice measures to teachers, the availability of a data system that would permit tracking individual students over time and linking students to their mathematics or science teachers, and a sufficiently large number of schools and teachers to ensure adequate statistical power for detecting relationships between instructional practices and test scores. Three districts that had completed their five-year LSC programs between 1998 and 2000 met these criteria and agreed to participate in the study.

The study focused on elementary and middle schools, because most of the systemic reforms were initially targeted at these grade levels (Shields, Corcoran, and Zucker, 1994; Porter et al., 1994; Goertz, 1999). Reform-oriented teaching at the high school level was not as fully implemented at the time the study began in 2000.

To maximize the chances that participating schools were balanced across a range of characteristics, we conducted a purposive sampling of schools. This sampling resulted in an oversampling of schools serving a larger proportion of students eligible for free or reduced-price lunches than for the districts as a whole. Each district encouraged eligible schools to participate, and schools received a $200 honorarium for participating.

Table 2.1 shows the school sample during the three years in which the main data collection took place. For analytic purposes, the goal was to include at least 20 schools in each cohort. However, in Cohort 2, the district had fewer than 20 schools at the targeted level. The number of schools varied slightly over the three years for two main reasons: Districts reconfigured some schools, and we eliminated schools in which all teachers declined to participate.

The specific grades and subjects were selected in consultation with district staff, to try to maximize the variability of reform-oriented instruction—i.e., we selected grades in which reform practices were widely used but did not yet reach complete implementation. Selection of grades was also constrained by the need to follow students over a three-year period, which was best accomplished if students did not cross school levels during the study (i.e., did not move from elementary to middle school).

The final sample included five grade-subject cohorts: two cohorts in middle school mathematics, and one cohort each in middle school science, elementary school mathematics, and elementary school science (see Table 2.1). The elementary school cohorts were enrolled in third grade in 2001–2002, the initial year of the study (referred to as year 1). The middle school science cohort and one of the middle school mathematics cohorts were enrolled in sixth grade; the other middle school

Table 2.1
Description of Participating Schools and Grade-Subject Cohorts

| Cohort | District | Subject | Year 1 (2001–2002) | | Year 2 (2002–2003) | | Year 3 (2003–2004) | |
|---|---|---|---|---|---|---|---|---|
| | | | Grade Studied | School Sample | Grade Studied | School Sample | Grade Studied | School Sample |
| 1 | 1 | Mathematics | 3 | 18 | 4 | 20 | 5 | 24 |
| 2 | 1 | Mathematics | 7 | 11 | 8 | 13 | 9 | 13 |
| 3 | 2 | Mathematics | 6 | 30 | 7 | 25 | 8 | 24 |
| 4 | 2 | Science | 3 | 20 | 4 | 21 | 5 | 21 |
| 5 | 3 | Science | 6 | 26 | 7 | 28 | 8 | 25 |

mathematics cohort was enrolled in seventh grade. We followed these students for two additional years, including 2002–2003 (referred to as year 2) and 2003–2004 (referred to as year 3).

The total number of schools per district across years and districts ranged from a low of 13 in Cohort 2 to a high of 57 in Cohort 1 (not shown). To achieve adequate statistical power to detect a non-zero relationship between instructional practices and student achievement, we sampled a different proportion of schools in each district, ranging from 35 percent (i.e., Cohort 1) to 100 percent (i.e., Cohort 2) of the schools in the districts. To minimize the variability in our final estimates, we selected samples that were uniformly distributed with respect to aggregate demographic and socioeconomic status variables. As a result, the school samples were representative of the district as a whole with respect to these student characteristics. Schools were located primarily within suburban and urban areas. More information about school demographics can be found in Appendix 2-A. In Cohorts 1 and 5, the student population was equally split between minority and white students. Cohort 2 contained predominantly white students (68 percent across the three years), whereas Cohorts 3 and 4 contained primarily minority students (approximately 70 to 75 percent). Close to one-half of the students in Cohorts 3 and 4 were eligible to receive free or reduced-price lunches (FRL). The proportion of FRL students was slightly higher in Cohort 1 (65 percent) and lower in Cohorts 2 and 5 (close to 40 and 20 percent, respectively).

Student sample sizes are shown by year in Table 2.2. The numbers in the table represent a comprehensive count of students in a given year. That is, they include any student who appeared in the cohort during that particular year, including students who moved into the district or students who were retained from a higher grade.

**Table 2.2**
**Student Samples**

| Cohort | Year 1 | Year 2 | Year 3 |
|--------|--------|--------|--------|
| 1 | 1,642 | 1,928 | 1,649 |
| 2 | 3,521 | 3,511 | 3,459 |
| 3 | 1,998 | 2,451 | 3,043 |
| 4 | 960 | 1,159 | 1,195 |
| 5 | 5,808 | 6,403 | 7,455 |

## Data Collection: Student-Achievement Data

Each district provided student-achievement scores on state tests and locally administered district tests from 2001 to 2003. In addition to mathematics and science scores, we also collected data on reading, writing, and language achievement tests. Scores in these other subjects are used in the statistical models as covariates to control for prior student achievement. All cohorts except Cohort 4 provided student test scores obtained one year before the data-collection efforts. These scores are referred to as "year 0" scores and are also used as covariates in the models.[1]

We could not rely solely on state and district tests for our longitudinal analysis, because these tests were not administered in every grade. Thus, we supplemented the state and district tests with the SAT-9, published by Harcourt Assessment. For each cohort, we administered multiple-choice (MC) SAT-9 tests in mathematics or science, as relevant. In three cohorts, we also administered SAT-9 tests in reading and language. The SAT-9 reading and language scores complemented the

---

[1] Achievement measures from year 0 serve as a baseline for this study. However, it is important to note that students were likely to have been exposed to reform-oriented instruction in or before year 0, so our study may be underestimating the effects of reform-oriented instruction.

reading and language scores provided by the districts and were used in our modeling to control for prior achievement. We also administered open-ended (OE) measures in one mathematics cohort and in both science cohorts. On the OE mathematics section, students responded to nine questions related to a particular topic or theme (Harcourt Assessment, 1996b); on the OE science section, students responded to nine tasks tied to one or two scenarios that assessed life, earth, and physical sciences (Harcourt Assessment, 1996a).[2] In addition, in one of the mathematics cohorts, we included in our analyses two SAT-9 MC subscale scores: problem solving (PS) and procedures (PR). PS assesses the skills and knowledge needed to solve mathematics problems. PR assesses students' ability to select and apply appropriate rules and strategies to arithmetic problems (see http://harcourtassessment.com). Tables 2.3a and b show the types of measures obtained at each cohort for each year. Distributions of scores for each year are provided in Appendix 2-B.

## Data Collection: Teacher Background and Classroom Practice Data

An expanded effort to measure classroom practice is a key feature of the Mosaic II study. This effort entailed using multiple methods to derive measures of the extent to which teachers were incorporating reform-oriented principles into their curriculum and instruction. During the first three years of the study, we used a survey, classroom logs, and a set of vignette-based questions to determine the extent to which

---

[2] The extent to which the externally administered SAT-9 is aligned with the curriculum of the districts in our study is unknown. However, research has found that students' performance can be influenced by test-curriculum alignment (Anderson, 2002; Gamoran et al., 1997; Schmidt and McKnight, 1995). The issue of alignment will be revisited in Chapter Four.

Table 2.3a
**Achievement Information Obtained for Each Cohort, Years 0 and 1**

| | Year 0 | | | Year 1 | | |
| Cohort | Tests | Subject(s) Tested | Format | Tests | Subject(s) Tested | Format |
|---|---|---|---|---|---|---|
| 1 | District | Math<br>Reading | MC<br>MC | SAT-9 | Math<br>Reading<br>Language | MC<br>MC<br>MC |
| 2 | District | Math<br>Reading | MC<br>MC | SAT-9 | Math<br>Reading<br>Language | MC<br>MC<br>MC |
| 3 | State | Math<br>Reading<br>Writing | MC<br>MC<br>MC | SAT-9 | Math[a]<br>Science | MC, OE<br>MC |
| 4 | | | | SAT-9 | Math[a]<br>Science | MC, OE<br>MC |
| 5 | District | Math<br>Reading | MC<br>MC | State | Math<br>Reading<br>Language | MC<br>MC<br>MC |
| | State | Science | MC | SAT-9 | Science | MC |

NOTES: All subjects were assessed solely with multiple-choice tests unless otherwise indicated.
[a] Mathematics Problem Solving and Mathematics Procedures subscale scores are available.

reform-oriented teaching practices were being used. The instruments were designed to provide overlapping evidence about the extent of the reform-oriented teaching that was occurring. All eligible teachers were asked to respond to the surveys, logs, and vignettes. In addition, we supplemented the main data-collection procedures with observations and interviews to provide context about teachers' responses on the surveys, logs, and vignettes. The observations and interviews were conducted with a smaller subset of teachers. Table 2.4 describes the data-collection instruments employed. The instruments are described in more detail in the following sections.

**Table 2.3b**
**Achievement Information Obtained for Each Cohort, Years 2 and 3**

| Cohort | Year 2 | | | Year 3 | | |
|---|---|---|---|---|---|---|
| | Tests | Subject(s) Tested | Format | Subject(s) Tests | Subject(s) Tested | Format |
| 1 | SAT-9 | Math<br>Reading<br>Language | MC<br>MC<br>MC | SAT-9 | Math<br>Reading<br>Language | MC<br>MC<br>MC |
| 2 | SAT-9 | Math<br>Reading<br>Language | MC<br>MC<br>MC | SAT-9 | Math<br>Reading<br>Language | MC<br>MC<br>MC |
| 3 | SAT-9 | Math[a]<br>Science | MC<br>MC, OE | SAT-9 | Math[a]<br>Science | MC, OE<br>MC |
| 4 | SAT-9 | Math[a]<br>Science | MC<br>MC, OE | SAT-9 | Math[a]<br>Science | MC<br>MC, OE |
| 5 | SAT-9 | Science | MC | SAT-9 | Science | MC, OE |

NOTES: All subjects were assessed solely with multiple-choice tests unless otherwise indicated.
[a] Mathematics Problem Solving and Mathematics Procedures subscale scores are available.

**Teacher Survey**

The teacher survey included questions about the teacher's educational background and experience, the mathematics or science curriculum taught in the class, and the use of a variety of teaching practices. Teachers indicated how much class time was spent on various mathematical or science topics (e.g., statistics, motion and forces) and the frequency with which they engaged in particular instructional activities (e.g., lecturing or introducing content through formal presentations, requiring students to explain their reasoning when giving an answer). They also indicated the frequency with which students took part in specific learning activities (e.g., answering worksheet questions, working on extended investigations). Questions of these types have been used extensively in research on mathematics and science instruction (see, e.g., Cohen and Hill, 2000; Hamilton et al., 2003; and Wenglinsky, 2002).

**Table 2.4**
**Description of Data-Collection Instruments**

| Data-Collection Instrument | Year(s) Collected | Provides Information About: |
|---|---|---|
| Teacher Survey | 1, 2, 3 | Teaching experience; curriculum coverage; professional development; instructional practices; teacher background information |
| Teacher Log | 1, 2, 3 | Amount of time spent on reform-oriented activities (e.g., discussing ideas, groupwork) and non-reform-oriented activities (e.g., working on worksheets) |
| Vignettes | 1, 2, 3 | Teachers' propensity to engage in reform instruction |
| Classroom Observations | 2 | Teachers' emphasis on inquiry and problem solving; holistic rating of the extent to which the lesson embodied reform principles |
| Teacher Interviews | 3 | Teachers' philosophy about mathematics and science instruction; influences on instruction; types of professional development activities |
| Cognitive Interviews | 4 | Teachers' interpretations of selected vignette-based items; understanding of reform-oriented instruction |

We created separate surveys for mathematics and science teachers each year, although many of the background items were identical across subjects. Surveys were pilot-tested locally and with teachers in each cohort, via telephone. Samples of surveys can be found in Appendix 2-C.

**Teacher Logs**

Each day during a two- to five-day period, teachers were asked to fill out a log describing specific activities that occurred during their mathematics or science lessons. While the surveys focused on long-term patterns of behavior, the logs focused on activities during a specific period.[3] Teachers indicated how much time students spent on selected activities (e.g., read from the textbook or other materials, explain their thinking

---

[3] In the first year of the study, we collected logs for five days. In the remaining two years, we collected logs for two days.

about mathematics or scientific ideas). Similarly, they indicated how much time they themselves devoted to selected behaviors (e.g., monitor students as they work, ask questions of individuals to test for understanding). Finally, teachers indicated the frequency with which certain activities occurred during the lesson (e.g., students engaged in a debate or discussion; teacher or student connected the topic to another subject, such as social studies). Copies of the forms for the teacher logs are provided as Appendix 2-D.

### Vignette-Based Items

As part of the survey, teachers were presented with two written vignettes, each consisting of four hypothetical classroom situations related to the teaching of specific mathematics or science topics. For each situation, the teacher was presented with a list of options describing possible actions that could be taken in response. Teachers indicated the likelihood that they would undertake each action. We interpreted responses to the vignettes as an indication of teachers' propensity to engage in reform-oriented instruction. More details about the development and scoring of the vignettes can be found in Chapter Three.

Table 2.5 indicates the number of teachers who responded to the surveys or logs. We obtained a roster of eligible teachers from each school, and all teachers in each year's subject–grade level combination at the designated schools were asked to participate. We provided teachers with a $100 honorarium to respond to the surveys and logs. Across the three years, response rates varied from 64 to 100 percent for mathematics teachers and from 55 to 99 percent for science teachers.

### Classroom Observations

In the second year of data collection, we observed classrooms to obtain an independent measure of the extent to which teachers engaged in reform-oriented instruction. To create the observation protocol, we identified elements of reform-oriented instruction that we thought were readily observable and would provide indicators of reform-oriented practices. The observation protocol consisted of 16 or 17 items that encompassed a variety of teacher and student activities, including

**Table 2.5**
**Teacher Survey and Log Response Rate**

| | Year 1 | | Year 2 | | Year 3 | |
|---|---|---|---|---|---|---|
| Cohort | Teacher Response (*n/N*) | Response Rate (%) | Teacher Response (*n/N*) | Response Rate (%) | Teacher Response (*n/N*) | Response Rate (%) |
| 1 | 68/82 | 82 | 80/86 | 93 | 71/89 | 80 |
| 2 | 43/63 | 68 | 64/96 | 67 | 57/81 | 71 |
| 3 | 64/99 | 64 | 43/43 | 100 | 38/41 | 93 |
| 4 | 69/124 | 55 | 67/68 | 99 | 65/69 | 94 |
| 5 | 67/85 | 79 | 75/85 | 88 | 68/91 | 75 |

NOTES: *n* refers to the number who completed the data-collection instruments. *N* refers to the total number of teachers eligible for inclusion in the study.

participation in groupwork, the kind of activities students participated in, the types of questions teachers asked, and the extent to which problem solving and inquiry were requested by teachers. For each item, the observation protocol described the activity and gave specific examples of the kinds of behaviors that would be considered an instance of high, medium, or low implementation of the activity.

Classroom observations were conducted during the second year of the study. Because of limited resources, we focused on one mathematics cohort and one science cohort. Three math observers and two science observers received training on how to use the observation protocols. After they were trained, each observed teachers once during a two-week observation period. Thirty-nine fourth-grade mathematics teachers from 13 schools from Cohort 1 were observed, as were 23 seventh-grade science teachers from 13 schools from Cohort 5. All teachers but one were rated by a single observer.[4] Teachers were paid a $50 honorarium for participating. For each item, observers first assigned a broad rating of high, medium, or low, and then subdivided that rating

---

[4] For this teacher, we averaged the observation ratings across the two raters. Raters tended to give similar scores, assigning ratings within one point of each other 80 percent of the time.

into one of three levels, creating a nine-point scale. Observers also gave a written justification for each of their ratings. Appendix 2-E provides the observation protocol for mathematics.

## Teacher Interviews

During the third year, we conducted in-depth interviews with 30 teachers to better understand the contextual influences on teachers' practices. We randomly selected three schools within each cohort, then randomly chose at least two teachers within each school. Obtaining information from teachers within the same school was intended to provide some information about the extent to which reform-oriented concepts were adopted within schools. In all, 30 teachers were interviewed across the five cohorts (see Table 2.6). Teachers received a $100 honorarium for their time.

We developed a semistructured interview protocol to gather information from teachers about the influence of local systemic reforms and other policies on their practices. Each interview lasted approximately 45 minutes and was conducted and recorded over the phone. The interview protocols included questions regarding factors likely to affect teachers' engagement in reform instruction, including school context and professional communities (McLaughlin and Talbert, 1993), pro-

**Table 2.6**
**Number of Teachers Participating in Interviews**

| Cohort | Subject | Grade | Number of Teachers Interviewed | |
|--------|---------|-------|--------|--------|
| | | | Year 3 | Year 4 |
| 1 | Mathematics | 5 | 5 | 9 |
| 2 | Mathematics | 9 | 5 | 6 |
| 3 | Mathematics | 8 | 8 | 5 |
| 4 | Science | 5 | 4 | 5 |
| 5 | Science | 8 | 8 | 6 |

fessional development (Corcoran, Shields, and Zucker, 1998; Supovitz, Mayer, andKahle, 2000), and state-mandated testing and accountability requirements (Cimbricz, 2002).

## Cognitive Interviews

In the fourth year of the study, we conducted cognitive interviews to gain insight into whether teachers' understanding of the vignette items matched our own. We recontacted participating year 3 teachers and solicited volunteers for the follow-up cognitive interviews. Teachers were offered a $100 honorarium and asked to contact the researchers to schedule a time for a telephone interview. The first five to eight teachers in each of the five grade-subject cohorts who responded were interviewed (see Table 2.6), which resulted in a total of 30 teachers interviewed—19 mathematics teachers and 11 science teachers.

We created five semistructured interview protocols corresponding to each of the subject–grade level cohorts. The scripts consisted of both a think-aloud portion and verbal probing. In the think-aloud portion, teachers were asked to verbalize their thought processes while answering vignette items. Teachers were encouraged to provide a running commentary, particularly as it related to the clarity of the vignettes and their understanding of an item's intent. In the verbal-probing portion, respondents were further queried about their reasons for choosing or rejecting particular teaching actions; the circumstances under which they would engage in certain behaviors; the perceived differences between selected teaching actions; the effects that certain contextual elements (such as district policy) had on their choice; and the absence of any relevant response options. Interviews lasted from 40 to 120 minutes, with most interviews taking approximately 90 minutes.

# CHAPTER THREE

# Measures of Teaching Practices

This chapter provides more information about the derivation and quality of the measures of instructional practices. We pay particular attention to the vignette-based measures, which were one of the innovative aspects of the study. The discussion begins with measures derived from the surveys and logs, then describes measures derived from the observations, and concludes with measures derived from the vignettes. For the most part, all the survey, logs, and vignette-based measures were available for all three years of the study; observational measures were available for only a sample of teachers in year 2.

## Measures Derived from Surveys and Logs

Drawing on data from teachers' responses to the surveys and logs, we grouped items together to create scales—i.e., measures of different aspects of instructional practice, curriculum coverage, teacher training and background, and classroom context. Measures of instructional practices, particularly measures of reform-oriented instruction, are the key independent variables in our analysis, but we were also interested in understanding other factors that might be related to achievement outcomes. Thus, we explore the effects of curriculum coverage, teacher training and background, and classroom context. Table 3.1 contains a list of the scales created from the surveys and logs. The complete set of items that make up each scale is presented in Appendix 3-A.

**Table 3.1**
**List of Scales Created from the Surveys and Logs**

| Scale | Data Source | Subject | Scale Metric |
|---|---|---|---|
| 1. Instructional Practice | | | |
| Reform Practices | Survey | Mathematics Science | 5-point Likert |
| Reform Relative to Text | Survey | Mathematics | 3-point Likert |
| Mathematical Processes | Survey | Mathematics | 5-point scale |
| Experiments | Survey | Science | 4-point Likert |
| Hours of Weekly Instruction | Survey | Mathematics Science | Continuous |
| Discussion | Log | Mathematics Science | 5-point Likert |
| Groupwork | Log | Mathematics Science | Continuous |
| Mixed-Ability Groupwork | Log | Mathematics Science | Continuous |
| Problem-Solving Groupwork | Log | Mathematics Science | Groupwork |
| Average Reform Activities | Log | Mathematics Science | 3-point Likert |
| Time on Task | Log | Mathematics Science | Continuous |
| Hands-On | Log | Science | Continuous |
| Seatwork | Log | Mathematics Science | 5-point Likert |
| Class Size | Log | Mathematics Science | Continuous |
| Materials Availability | Survey | Mathematics Science | 4-point Likert |
| 2. Curriculum Coverage | | | |
| Operations | Survey | Mathematics | 5-point Likert |
| Algebra | Survey | Mathematics | 5-point Likert |

**Table 3.1—Continued**

| Scale | Data Source | Subject | Scale Metric |
|---|---|---|---|
| | 2. Curriculum Coverage—Continued | | |
| Earth Science | Survey | Science | 6-point Likert |
| Life Science | Survey | Science | 6-point Likert |
| Physical Science | Survey | Science | 6-point Likert |
| Reasoning and Technology | Survey | Science | 6-point Likert |
| Science Content | Survey | Science | 6-point Likert |
| Kits | Survey | Science | 6-point Likert |
| Sleuths | Survey | Science | Continuous |
| | 3. Classroom Context | | |
| Heterogeneous Classroom | Survey | Science | Dichotomous |
| Class Size | Log | Mathematics Science | Continuous |
| Materials Availability | Survey | Mathematics Science | 4-point Likert |
| | 4. Teacher Background | | |
| Professional Development | Survey | Mathematics Science | 5-point Likert |
| Experience | Survey | Mathematics Science | Continuous |
| Experience at Grade | Survey | Mathematics | Continuous |
| Master's Degree | Survey | Mathematics Science | Dichotomous |
| Math Degree | Survey | Mathematics Science | 3-point scale |
| Science Degree | Survey | Mathematics Science | 3-point scale |
| Confidence | Survey | Mathematics Science | Dichotomous |

**Instructional Practice Scales**

We created five Instructional Practice scales from the surveys:

- *Reform Practices* is composed of nine items measuring the frequency with which teachers engaged in reform-oriented instructional practices relating to student activities (e.g., groupwork), student assignments (e.g., extended investigations), and teacher questioning techniques (e.g., use of open-ended questions). The items on this scale are similar to those used in other research on mathematics and science reform, including some national longitudinal surveys (Cohen and Hill, 2000; Hamilton et al., 2003; Swanson and Stevenson, 2002; Wenglinsky, 2002).

- *Reform Relative to Text* is a five-item mathematics scale assessing how teachers' emphasis on certain reform practices compared with that of their primary textbook. Examples of reform practices measured on this scale include the extent to which teachers incorporated manipulatives (i.e., hands-on tools or objects meant to represent mathematics ideas) into the lessons and the extent to which teachers required explanations and justifications from their students.

- *Mathematical Processes* measure teachers' self-reported emphases on proof and justifications, problem solving, mathematical communication, connections, and mathematical representations. These are aspects of mathematics emphasized by the NCTM *Standards* (1989, 2000).

- *Experiments* is a four-item science scale describing teachers' emphasis on inquiry-based activities, such as collecting data, making observations, conducting a controlled investigation, and carrying out a planned experiment.

- *Hours of Weekly Instruction* represents teachers' estimation of the number of hours of mathematics or science instruction students received in a typical week.

The remaining eight Instructional Practice scales were derived from the logs:

- *Discussion* is a four-item scale based on teachers' reports of class time spent in dialogue and on facilitation of student thinking. The scale consists of two items measuring the time students spent explaining their thinking and leading discussions, and two items measuring the amount of time teachers spent discussing solutions to open-ended questions and asking students questions to test for understanding.
- *Groupwork* measures teachers' self-reports of the number of minutes students spent working in groups.
- *Mixed-Ability Groupwork* is derived from the Groupwork scale. It represents teachers' estimates of the proportion of time in which students worked in mixed-ability groups.
- *Problem-Solving Groupwork* is also created from the Groupwork scale. It measures teachers' self-reports of the proportion of time students spent in groups collaboratively solving new problems.
- *Average Reform Activities* is a six-item scale measuring the number of times teachers reported specific reform behaviors during the lesson. These behaviors include the frequency with which students debated ideas, made connections with other subject areas (e.g., social studies), and worked on novel problems.
- *Time on Task* is a measure of how many minutes teachers reported were effectively spent on mathematics or science instruction. It was derived by subtracting the number of minutes spent on administrative tasks or discipline problems from the total length of the class (in minutes).
- *Hands-On* consists of teachers' reports of the number of minutes the class spent on hands-on science.
- *Seatwork* describes teachers' reports of the class time students spent reading from the textbook or completing worksheets or problem sets. Seatwork is qualitatively different from the other Instructional Practice scales in that it does not directly address reform practices; instead, it focuses on more-conventional activities.

The scales are on a variety of metrics from dichotomous, to Likert, to continuous. For scales that use a *dichotomously* scored item, a score of 1 indicates the presence or existence of the construct measured by that scale, and a score of 0 indicates an absence of that construct. For measures that use a Likert scale, the score is the average response across items, with higher scores denoting more-frequent use of the practices measured by that scale. A score of 5 on the Reform Practices scale, for instance, indicates that teachers spent much time on reform-oriented activities. In contrast, a score of 1 on this scale indicates that teachers spent little time on reform-oriented instruction. Other Likert-based scales are interpreted in an analogous fashion. For *continuously* scored scales, the teacher's response represents the score on that measure. Thus, a score of 20 on the Hands-On scale indicates that the teacher reported 20 minutes of instruction on hands-on science.

Our study relies on naturally occurring variation in teacher practices to examine the relationship between classroom practice and student test scores. That is, the design assumes that there is substantial variation in the instructional practices among teachers within a school, even though teachers may have been exposed to the same training. To determine whether our assumption was true, we examined whether there was a sufficient level of variability on the instructional-practice measures. Tables 3.2a–c provide the descriptive statistics for the instructional-practice measures across years for Cohort 1. Appendix 3-B provides the statistics for the other cohorts. An examination of the descriptive statistics indicates that, within each cohort, most Instructional Practice scales showed moderate variability. Even within the same school, we found variation in the classroom practices of teachers.

We also examined the reliability or internal consistency estimates of the measures used (i.e., the extent to which items of the same scale assess the same construct). It is important to examine the internal consistency estimates, because more-reliable measures allow for better detection of relationships. As shown in Tables 3.2a–c, the majority of the scales have adequate reliability, typically above .60. The few scales that had been identified as having internal consistency estimates below .60 in one year (e.g., Seatwork) also tend to have much higher estimates in another year, suggesting that the low estimates may have been due to anomalous response patterns particular to a certain set of teachers within a given year. Thus, we retained all scales in our analyses.

**Table 3.2a**
**Characteristics of Scales for Instructional Practices, Curriculum Coverage, Teacher Background, and Classroom Context for Cohort 1, Year 1**

| Scale | Year 1 | | | | | |
|---|---|---|---|---|---|---|
| | *N* | Mean | SD | Min | Max | Alpha |
| Instructional Practices | | | | | | |
| Reform-High | 68 | 0.00 | 1.00 | –2.82 | 2.63 | .75 |
| Reform-Full | 68 | 1.93 | .59 | .60 | 3.09 | .85 |
| Reform Practices | 68 | 3.81 | .47 | 2.44 | 4.78 | .72 |
| Reform Relative to Text | 68 | 2.38 | .41 | 1.40 | 3.00 | .63 |
| Mathematical Processes | — | — | — | — | — | — |
| Hours of Weekly Instruction | — | — | — | — | — | — |
| Discussion | 63 | 2.45 | .59 | 1.50 | 4.55 | .77 |
| Groupwork | 63 | 11.27 | 9.26 | .00 | 36.00 | — |
| Mixed-Ability Groupwork | 62 | 6.38 | 7.92 | .00 | 36.00 | — |
| Problem-Solving Groupwork | 62 | 5.51 | 7.76 | .00 | 36.00 | — |
| Average Reform Activities | — | — | — | — | — | — |
| Time on Task | 63 | 43.03 | 11.91 | 21.60 | 78.40 | — |
| Seatwork | 63 | 2.58 | .77 | 1.00 | 4.30 | .58 |
| Curriculum | | | | | | |
| Operations | 67 | 3.78 | .82 | 2.00 | 5.00 | .64 |
| Algebra | — | — | — | — | — | — |
| Teacher Background | | | | | | |
| Professional Development | 68 | 2.53 | .87 | 1.00 | 4.86 | .88 |
| Experience | 68 | 13.28 | 9.61 | 1.00 | 37.00 | — |
| Experience at Grade | 68 | 5.54 | 4.51 | 1.00 | 20.00 | — |
| Classroom Context | | | | | | |
| Class Size | 63 | 22.95 | 3.66 | 11.60 | 30.80 | — |

**Table 3.2a—Continued**

| Scale | N | Mean | SD | Min | Max | Alpha |
|---|---|---|---|---|---|---|
| | | | Year 1 | | | |
| | Observations | | | | | |
| Deep Understanding | — | — | — | — | — | — |
| Overall Reform | — | — | — | — | — | — |

NOTES: N = number of teachers; SD = standard deviation; Min = minimum; Max = maximum; Alpha = reliability estimate of internal consistency.

**Table 3.2b**
**Characteristics of Scales for Instructional Practices, Curriculum Coverage, Teacher Background, and Classroom Context for Cohort 1, Year 2**

| Scale | N | Mean | SD | Min | Max | Alpha |
|---|---|---|---|---|---|---|
| | | | Year 2 | | | |
| | Instructional Practices | | | | | |
| Reform-High | 80 | 0.00 | 1.00 | −3.11 | 2.00 | .80 |
| Reform-Full | 77 | 1.47 | .54 | .34 | 2.90 | .86 |
| Reform Practices | 80 | 3.71 | .47 | 2.56 | 4.44 | .73 |
| Reform Relative to Text | 80 | 3.91 | .47 | 1.40 | 3.00 | .64 |
| Mathematical Processes | 80 | 2.36 | .44 | .00 | 5.00 | .75 |
| Hours of Weekly Instruction | 80 | 6.70 | 2.32 | 3.00 | 20.00 | — |
| Discussion | 77 | 2.59 | .67 | 1.25 | 4.38 | .80 |
| Groupwork | 77 | 15.45 | 14.79 | .00 | 55.00 | — |
| Mixed-Ability Groupwork | 76 | 12.02 | 13.27 | .00 | 55.00 | — |
| Problem-Solving Groupwork | 75 | 10.55 | 12.19 | .00 | 55.00 | — |
| Average Reform  Activities | 77 | 1.94 | .35 | 1.08 | 2.83 | .64 |
| Time on Task | 78 | 46.56 | 12.40 | 20.00 | 82.50 | — |

**Table 3.2b—Continued**

| Scale | Year 2 | | | | | |
|---|---|---|---|---|---|---|
| | N | Mean | SD | Min | Max | Alpha |
| Curriculum | | | | | | |
| Operations | 79 | 3.85 | .84 | 2.00 | 5.00 | .63 |
| Algebra | 80 | 2.88 | .73 | 1.00 | 5.00 | .33 |
| Teacher Background | | | | | | |
| Professional Development | 80 | 2.32 | .82 | 1.00 | 4.86 | .87 |
| Experience | 80 | 13.33 | 9.67 | 1.00 | 35.00 | — |
| Experience at Grade | 80 | 5.54 | 5.14 | .00 | 23.00 | — |
| Classroom Context | | | | | | |
| Class Size | 78 | 25.03 | 3.51 | 14.00 | 32.00 | — |
| Observations | | | | | | |
| Deep Understanding | 38 | 3.10 | 2.08 | .20 | 7.80 | .87 |
| Overall Reform | 38 | 2.60 | 1.63 | .31 | 5.85 | .87 |

NOTES: N = number of teachers; SD = standard deviation; Min = minimum; Max = maximum; Alpha = reliability estimate of internal consistency.

**Table 3.2c**
**Characteristics of Scales for Instructional Practices, Curriculum Coverage, Teacher Background, and Classroom Context for Cohort 1, Year 3**

| Scale | Year 3 | | | | | |
|---|---|---|---|---|---|---|
| | N | Mean | SD | Min | Max | Alpha |
| Instructional Practices | | | | | | |
| Reform-High | 71 | 0.00 | 1.00 | −3.00 | 2.16 | .82 |
| Reform-Full | 71 | 1.87 | .59 | .75 | 3.12 | .85 |
| Reform Practices | 71 | 3.84 | .58 | 1.78 | 4.67 | .83 |
| Reform Relative to Text | 70 | 3.76 | 1.20 | 1.20 | 3.00 | .70 |
| Mathematical Processes | 70 | 2.32 | .43 | 1.00 | 5.00 | .58 |
| Hours of Weekly Instruction | 70 | 6.21 | 1.54 | 3.00 | 10.00 | — |
| Discussion | 69 | 2.41 | .64 | 1.50 | 4.75 | .74 |
| Groupwork | 69 | 13.29 | 12.96 | .00 | 52.50 | — |
| Mixed-Ability Groupwork | 68 | 10.32 | 12.13 | .00 | 52.50 | — |
| Problem-Solving Groupwork | 67 | 8.48 | 9.32 | .00 | 32.81 | — |
| Average Reform Activities | 69 | 1.88 | .41 | 1.04 | 2.83 | .77 |
| Time on Task | 69 | 50.53 | 11.62 | 20.00 | 85.00 | — |
| Seatwork | 69 | 2.52 | .82 | 1.00 | 4.00 | .31 |
| Curriculum | | | | | | |
| Operations | 70 | 3.56 | 1.20 | 2.00 | 5.00 | — |
| Algebra | 70 | 2.85 | .76 | 1.00 | 5.00 | .50 |

**Table 3.2c—Continued**

| Scale | Year 3 | | | | | |
|---|---|---|---|---|---|---|
| | N | Mean | SD | Min | Max | Alpha |
| Teacher Background | | | | | | |
| Professional Development | 71 | 2.54 | .88 | 1.00 | 4.86 | .87 |
| Experience | 70 | 12.29 | 8.77 | 1.00 | 35.00 | — |
| Experience at Grade | 71 | 6.24 | 5.29 | 1.00 | 20.00 | — |
| Classroom Context | | | | | | |
| Class Size | 69 | 26.20 | 3.57 | 9.50 | 33.00 | — |
| Observations | | | | | | |
| Deep Understanding | — | — | — | — | — | — |
| Overall Reform | — | — | — | — | — | — |

NOTES: *N* = number of teachers; SD = standard deviation; Min = minimum; Max = maximum; Alpha= reliability estimate of internal consistency.

### Curriculum Coverage Scales

Two scales, derived from the survey responses, are related to curriculum coverage for mathematics:

- *Operations* measures the number of weeks teachers reported spending on operations with whole numbers.
- *Algebra* measures the number of weeks teachers reported spending on algebraic topics. At the elementary grades, the topics focus on areas that develop number sense, such as patterns and functions. At the middle grades, these topics are traditional algebraic content areas (e.g., polynomials and rational numbers).

A total of seven Science scales relate to curriculum materials and content, all derived from the surveys:

- *Earth Science, Life Science, Physical Science,* and *Reasoning and Technology* assess the number of lessons teachers reported spending on the respective topic. These scales are present only at the elementary grades.

- *Science Content* measures the average number of lessons spent on particular topics. At the elementary grades, the topics are earth science, life science, physical science, and reasoning and technology. At the middle school grades, topics include disease, heredity, and motions and forces (see Appendix 3-A for a complete list of other topics used at the middle grades).

Two additional Science scales are related to the use of specific science materials that are believed to facilitate reform-oriented teaching and promote inquiry skills:

- *Kits* is an elementary-grade scale assessing the number of lessons teachers spent on guided curriculum materials that focus on investigative, hands-on activities.[1]
- *Sleuths* is a middle-grade scale measuring the number of lessons teachers spent on Science Sleuths. Science Sleuths are curricular materials that encourage students to solve "real-world" mysteries by conducting experiments and investigations in a "virtual science laboratory."

Tables 3.2a–c provide the descriptive statistics of curriculum-coverage measures for Cohort 1 (see Appendix 3-B for the descriptive statistics for the other cohorts). On average, teachers report fairly extensive coverage of operations and moderate coverage of algebra, although there is also much variation in teachers' responses. For the most part, adequate internal consistency estimates are also observed for both scales.

---

[1] We asked teachers about three specific science kits. The first kit was the Full Option Science System (FOSS) materials created by the Lawrence Hall of Science, University of California, Berkeley. The second was the Science and Technology for Children (STC) materials developed by the National Science Resources Center. The third was a curricular program created by the district participating in our study. All three programs are research-based and inquiry-centered. More information about the FOSS and STC programs can be found at http://lhsfoss.org/index.html and http://www.carolina.com/stc/.

**Teacher Background Scales**

We created seven scales, all derived from the surveys, about teacher background:

- *Professional Development* measures the amount of subject-specific in-service training received in the past 12 months in areas such as students' thinking, assessment, and mathematics or science standards.
- *Experience* indicates the total number of years teachers taught on a full-time basis.
- *Experience at Grade* indicates the total number of years teachers taught at the grade level they were currently assigned.
- *Master's Degree* assesses whether teachers had a master's degree in any subject.
- *Math Degree* and *Science Degree* indicate whether the teacher had an undergraduate major or minor in a mathematics- or science-intensive field.
- *Confidence* assesses whether or not teachers felt very confident in the mathematics or science topics that they were asked to teach.

Tables 3.2a–c shows the distribution for Teacher Background scales on a Likert or continuous metric for Cohort 1; Table 3.3 shows the distribution for the dichotomous Teacher Background scales (see Appendix 3-B for the Teacher Background results for the other cohorts). Across the three years, approximately 50 percent of Cohort 1 teachers report having a master's degree, and 50 to 60 percent report feeling very confident in the mathematics knowledge that they were asked to teach. On average, teachers have 13 years of total teaching experience, and five to six years of experience teaching at the grade to which they are currently assigned. Teachers also tend to have a moderate level of professional development training in the past 12 months. For all these teacher-background measures, we observed a sufficient level of variation to allow for modeling of relationships to student achievement.

**Table 3.3**
**Distribution of "Yes" Responses for Dichotomous Scales for Teacher Background and Classroom Context in Cohort 1**

| Scale | Year 1 | | Year 2 | | Year 3 | |
|---|---|---|---|---|---|---|
| | **N** | **Percentage** | **N** | **Percentage** | **N** | **Percentage** |
| Teacher Background | | | | | | |
| Master's Degree | 68 | 53 | 80 | 48 | 70 | 50 |
| Confidence | 66 | 50 | 80 | 60 | 70 | 60 |
| Classroom Context | | | | | | |
| Heterogeneous Classroom | 67 | 61 | 80 | 72 | 71 | 56 |

## Classroom Context Scales

The final set of survey scales is designed to provide context about classroom conditions:

- *Heterogeneous Classroom* is an indicator variable denoting whether or not the teacher reported in the survey that the classroom consisted of a mix of student abilities.
- *Class Size* is a measure of teachers' log reports of the number of students in the class.
- *Materials Availability* assesses teachers' survey reports of whether science tools, such as beakers and graduated cylinders, were readily available for use.

The distributions for the Classroom Context scales for Cohort 1 are provided in Tables 3.2 and 3.3 (Appendix 3-B provides analogous results for Cohorts 2 through 5). Teachers report an average class size of approximately 25 students; but some teachers have significantly smaller classes (around 10 students), and other teachers have significantly larger classes (approximately 33 students). There is also variability with respect to the percentage of teachers who responded that they taught in classrooms with a mixture of student-ability levels. Again, these results suggest a sufficient level of variation for modeling.

## Measures Derived from Observations

Two scales were created from the classroom observations during the second year of the study:

- *Deep Understanding* measures observers' ratings of the extent to which teachers emphasized problem solving or inquiry. Items on this scale focus on the extent to which teachers guided reasoning and problem solving, the extent to which students worked on complex problems that required analysis, and the extent to which the lesson had a sequence of activities that facilitated conceptual understanding.
- *Overall Reform* represents observers' holistic impression of the degree to which the lesson as a whole embodied reform principles. In addition to the items encompassed by Deep Understanding, Overall Reform consists of other aspects of reform-oriented instruction, including the extent to which teachers drew connections to other subject areas, the extent to which students worked in groups, and the extent to which students worked with hands-on activities or with manipulatives.

Classroom observations were conducted with approximately half of the teacher sample in Cohort 1. The two scales have very high internal consistency estimates and show variation in observers' ratings (see Tables 3.2a–c). The ratings suggest that observers judged teachers' teaching to be substantively more indicative of traditional pedagogy than was indicated by teachers' responses on the surveys and logs. This finding is consistent with the results of other studies (Mayer, 1999). Although there are a number of reasons for the differences between observers' ratings and teachers' responses (see Stecher, Le, et al., 2006) for a comprehensive discussion), one likely factor is that the observations were conducted for only one lesson, whereas the survey and log responses encompassed a broader time period. These differences should be kept in mind when interpreting relationships between measures derived from observations and those derived from surveys and logs.

## Vignette-Based Measures

The vignettes were the most innovative measure of instructional practice, and we describe their development in somewhat greater detail than we do the other measures. Additional information about development and validation is reported in Stecher, Le, et al. (2006) and Le et al. (2006). The following sections briefly describe the development of the vignette items, the computation of the vignette-based measures, and the results of analyses to validate the vignettes as indicators of reform-oriented instruction.

### Developing the Classroom Vignettes

Our purpose in using vignette-based items was to provide a behaviorally anchored indication of teachers' propensity to use reform-oriented instructional practices. Describing teaching options in terms of specific, situated behaviors avoids the problems of language and terminology that have been documented with surveys. Instead of using reform-oriented terminology, such as "mathematical or scientific communication," the vignette-based items attempt to describe a specific instructional situation and to present alternative teacher actions in neutral, behavioral terms.

The first step in developing the vignette-based items was to distill a list of reform-oriented instructional practices that could serve as a basis for vignette development. We convened panels of mathematicians, scientists, and mathematics and science educators to help in this process. Using the standards put forth by NRC, NCTM, and AAAS, the panel developed a taxonomy containing elements of reform-oriented mathematics and science curriculum and instruction organized into three or four major categories. In mathematics, the categories include the nature of mathematics, students' mathematical thinking, and mathematics instruction. In science, the categories include promoting scientific understanding, students' scientific thinking, classroom practices, and teacher knowledge (see Appendix 3-C).

The expert panel helped us frame the taxonomy in behavioral terms, drawing clear contrasts between the presence and absence of each element. They also provided benchmark descriptions of behaviors that were indicative of more and less reform teaching, as well as behaviors that were not associated with reform teaching. The non-reform behaviors include a variety of practices associated with other approaches that are not the focus of this study. Because many teachers are likely to engage in non–reform approaches, we include some of those practices within the response options to make the vignettes more representative of teachers' instruction.

Two vignettes were developed for each subject-grade combination. We chose topic areas within mathematics and science that were amenable to reform-oriented teaching and that represented prominent elements in the curriculum for the identified grade level in the participating districts. For example, the fourth-grade mathematics vignettes focus on perimeter and area and two-digit multiplication. A list of topics for each cohort can be found in Appendix 3-D. To ensure that the vignettes were appropriate to the course content of each grade and district, new vignettes were constructed each year.

### Structure of the Vignette-Based Items

A set of instructions preceded each vignette and included a general description of the scenarios and information about how teachers were to respond to the vignettes. These instructions were followed by a brief context section, which established a curricular setting for the specific vignette. The context section described the instructional objective of the unit, its length, and the relevant topics that had previously been covered. Teachers were told to assume that any other unspecified details were similar to their current school and current students.

Following the context section, each vignette contained four instructional problems that provided teachers with hypothetical classroom events at different points within the given mathematics or science unit. The instructional problems were selected as likely situations in which reform-oriented practices would be manifested. The first problem, "introducing the lesson," focused on the manner in which the teacher would begin the unit. Specifically, teachers were asked to indicate what kinds of activities they would use to introduce the lesson concept. The second problem, "responding to student error," involved teachers' responses to a student mistake that occurred in the middle of the unit. The third situation, "reconciling different approaches," involved teachers' reactions to students who described two different approaches to solving a problem, both of which were correct but differed in their efficiency or completeness. The final situation, "choosing learning objectives," addressed the learning objectives teachers would emphasize had they designed the unit (see Appendix 2-C for examples of the vignettes).[2]

After each instructional problem, teachers were presented with a list of options that reflected a range of teaching actions, from behaviors that were not associated with reform pedagogy (e.g., showing students how to follow a specific algorithm) to teacher behaviors that were consistent with reform-oriented teaching (e.g., asking students to discern the thinking behind an incorrect response). Teachers were asked to rate the likelihood of engaging in each option using a four-point scale from "very unlikely" to "very likely," or, for questions of emphasis, from "no emphasis" to "great emphasis." The vignettes were pilot-tested with teachers in the targeted grades from districts not participating in the project and were revised as necessary.

The two vignettes were designed to have options that were parallel across the different instructional problems. However, inherent differences in the content areas mean that some response options found in one vignette are not always replicable in another. This is particularly true in science, for which the diversity of the curriculum makes it difficult to create precisely parallel problems. For example, some science units involve hands-on investigations (i.e., experimental lessons), whereas others involve learning from books and other sources (i.e., observational lessons). We tried to reflect both of these kinds of learning activities in our vignettes so that they would be more representative of science teaching. However, we found that these two contexts do not lend themselves to similar teacher-response options, because concepts, variables, or procedures that are relevant in one setting do not have strict analogues in the other. For instance, in an experimental activity, students often fail to control for some irrelevant variable, and atten-

---

[2] The complete set of surveys for all subjects and grade levels, including the vignettes, is available at http://www.rand.org/education/projects/mosaic2/.

tion to this failure needs to be included among the teacher-response options. In an observational activity, there often is no analogous concern. These types of differences make it difficult to create parallel options and, as will be presented later in this chapter, may explain why teachers' responses in science are not as consistent as those observed in mathematics.

### Measures Derived from Vignettes

The first step in developing the vignette-based measures of reform-oriented instruction was to assign a value from 1 (nonreform) to 4 (high reform) to each response option. During the first year of the study, the expert panel was involved in establishing these ratings. In subsequent years, we used the decision guidelines the panel established to rate the responses. Four members of the research team independently rated each response option, then the four convened to reconcile differences. In some instances, it was decided that an option could not be scored unambiguously and these options were omitted from scoring. Options receiving a rating of 3 or 4 were classified as "indicative of high-reform-oriented teaching," and options receiving a rating of 1 or 2 were classified as "indicative of non-reform-oriented teaching." Across the three years and grade levels, between 43 and 60 percent of the mathematics options and between 45 and 57 percent of the science options were considered high-reform-oriented options.

Using teachers' responses to the vignette items, we created two vignette-based measures. The first measure, *Reform-High*, was based on only the high-reform-oriented options. Reform-High is the standardized sum of teachers' answers to all the high-reform-oriented response options across the two scenarios. Higher scores on this measure represent a greater propensity to select reform-oriented instructional approaches. Table 3.2 shows that there is variation on the Reform-High scale, and that it had a high internal consistency estimate.

The second measure, called *Reform-Full*, reflects responses to both the high- and low-reform-oriented options. We used multidimensional scaling to plot teachers' responses to all the options in three-dimensional space (see Stecher, Le, et al., 2006). We added into the scaling process two additional "ideal" teachers. The first represented a simulated consistently ideal high-reform-oriented teacher, whose responses corresponded exactly to our judgments of reform orientation. Conversely, the other represented a simulated consistently ideal non-reform-oriented teacher, whose responses were just the opposite. Reform-Full reflects variation on three dimensions, one of which relates to reform-oriented teaching. The elements that make up the other two dimensions are not fully known but are likely to include practices that are not the focus of this study. Reform-Full is derived by computing the Euclidean distance in three dimensions of each teacher from the simulated consistently high-reform teacher. We rescaled Reform-Full so that teachers who are closer to the consistently high-reform-oriented teacher received higher scores.

Figure 3.1 shows the derived distribution of teachers for fourth-grade mathematics from Cohort 1 in year 2. The plot is typical of the distributions for the other grades, years, and subjects. Each responding teacher in our sample is represented by a gray ball in the middle of the figure, while the idealized high-reform-oriented and non-reform-oriented teachers are represented by the balls on the far right and far left, respectively. The figure shows that teachers' responses to the vignettes were generally more similar to our idealized high-reform-oriented teacher than they were to our idealized non-reform-oriented teacher. This result is not surprising, given that we chose sites that were actively promoting reform-oriented teaching. However, it is also important to note that teachers show substantial variability in responses, which supports the ability to evaluate relationships between the vignette-based measures and student achievement (see Tables 3.2a–c).

### Validity of Vignette-Based Measures as Indicators of Reform-Oriented Instruction

We conducted further analyses of the validity of vignettes as measures of classroom instruction, because the use of vignettes as an analytic tool is much more recent and untried than the other measures. We examined the internal validity of the measures by exploring the extent to which correlations between teachers' responses to the vignettes conform to expectations. We examined external validity by inspecting correlations of the vignette-based scales with the survey, log, and observation scales. Finally, we collected qualitative evidence regarding the extent to which teachers interpreted the vignette items in the manner that we had intended. The results below are based on fourth-grade mathematics classes in Cohort 1, for which we had the largest number of classroom observations. Mathematics results from other grades and cohorts are generally similar to those presented here. Science results are similar, although the relationships were somewhat weaker.

**Figure 3.1**
**Distribution of Teachers' Responses in Relation to Idealized Low- and High-Reform-Oriented Teachers, Cohort 1, Year 2**

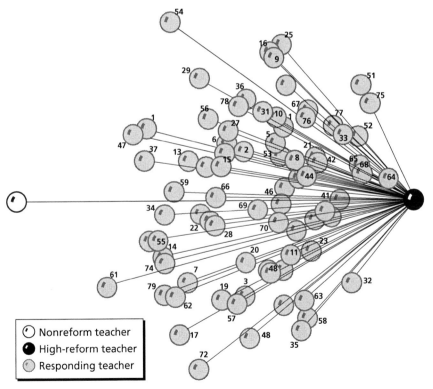

NOTE: The numbers in the figure represent teacher identification codes.
RAND MG480-3.1

**Internal Validity.** Our conception posits that teachers' tendencies to engage in reform-oriented teaching remain relatively stable or consistent across different content areas. If this assumption were true, we would expect items that were designed to be comparable to elicit similar responses across the two vignettes. It is important to note that teachers' responses can be consistent across the two vignettes, yet represent a mixture of nonreform-, low-reform-, and high-reform-oriented behaviors. Results indicate that teachers' responses to pairs of comparable response options are moderately to substantially similar in about one-half of the cases in mathematics, but in less than one-quarter of the cases in science.[3] These findings are consistent with our experience of developing the vignettes, in which comparable options were much more difficult to achieve in science than in mathematics.

If reform-oriented teaching is a stable aspect of teachers' instruction (as the item-level analyses suggest), we would also expect correlations between similar problems that were set in different contexts to be larger than correlations between dissimilar problems set in the same context. Again, the fourth-grade mathematics results conform to expectations. For instance, the correlation between the "responding to student error" problems across the two different scenarios is generally higher than the correlations between the "responding to student error" problem and other instructional problems within the same scenario. This result suggests that the vignettes were measuring relatively stable aspects of reform-oriented teaching.

Given that the vignettes were measuring relatively stable aspects of reform-oriented teaching, we combined the pairs of problem-level scores across the two scenarios to create four composite scores. In fourth-grade mathematics, the correlations among these four problem-based composites ranged from .22 to .53. These moderate correlations justify our decision to combine the four composites into overall measures of reform orientation (i.e., Reform-Full and Reform-High).

---

[3] We conducted this analysis using weighted kappa statistics. Such statistics are a measure of the agreement between independent ratings after adjusting for the level of agreement that would occur by chance alone. Using the guidelines put forth by Landis and Koch (1977), we label kappa values below .20 as "slight," from .21 to .40 as "fair," from .41 to .60 as "moderate," and higher than .60 as "substantial."

**External Validity.** Another way to look at the validity of the vignettes is to examine the degree to which the vignette-based measures show the expected relationships with other measures of reform-oriented teaching derived from the surveys, logs, and observations. We selected six scales from the surveys, logs, and observations that we believed would be either strongly positively correlated or not at all correlated with reform-oriented teaching: Mathematical Processes, Reform Practices, Discussion, Seatwork, Deep Understanding, and Overall Reform. With the exception of Seatwork, we expected all these scales to be positively related to the vignette measures. Seatwork is measuring an aspect of instruction that has been associated with more-traditional practices, and empirical studies have found reform-oriented and traditional instruction to be uncorrelated (Hamilton et al., 2003). Thus, we expected Seatwork to be uncorrelated with Reform-High and Reform-Full.

For the most part, the measures behave as predicted (see Appendix 3-E, Table 3-E.1, for correlations among the vignette-based scales, and selected survey, log, and observation measures for fourth-grade mathematics). Seatwork is uncorrelated with the other measures of reform practices, which is consistent with the premise that traditional and reform-oriented practices are orthogonal dimensions. The survey and log measures of reform-oriented practices are positively correlated to each other as well as to Reform-High. The Reform-Full scale is positively related to the two observational scales of reform-oriented practices and is unrelated to the Seatwork scale, all as predicted. However, not all predicted relationships were found. Reform-Full is not positively correlated with the other log and survey measures of reform-oriented practice. This pattern of relationships suggests that the Reform-Full scale and the observational scales may be measuring some aspect of practice that is not well represented in the Reform-High scale and in the survey and log scales.

Taken together, the empirical analyses provide some qualified support for the validity of vignettes as indicators of reform-oriented instruction. The item-level analysis and the patterns of correlations among the problem-level scores suggest that reform-oriented teaching is a stable aspect of teachers' instruction. That Reform-High shows significant associations with the surveys and logs measures but not with the observational measures, whereas Reform-Full shows the opposite patterns, suggests that Reform-High and Reform-Full may be measuring different aspects of reform-oriented teaching. Reform-High was constructed using only those response options deemed to be indicative of high-reform instruction. It is a linear combination of these options, much as the survey- and log-based measures are linear combinations of responses to multiple reform items. Reform-Full, in contrast, is a multidimensional scale made up of all vignette items, and it reflects some combination of reform-oriented and other practices. Although we do not know what elements of practice characterize the other dimensions that are present in Reform-Full, it is possible that they were also apparent to observers and are present in observers' ratings of practice.

**Qualitative Validity Evidence.** Another important facet of the validity of vignettes is the extent to which teachers' interpretations of instructional-practice items match the intentions of the developers (Desimone and Le Floch, 2004). Differences in interpretation can provide erroneous depictions of what occurs in the classroom, so it is important to confirm that teachers and researchers have a common understanding of the meaning of the items and responses.

Cognitive interviews with 30 teachers in which they verbalized their thought processes while responding to the vignette items clearly indicate that teachers' understanding of the vignettes and the options matched our own. In 84 percent of the cases, teachers' interpretations of vignette items agreed with our intentions. In a few cases, they did not, and the cognitive interviews shed light on the discrepancies. For example, teachers assumed that some options included other activities that were not described, and they thus responded to the broader set of behaviors they thought made more sense. Similarly, despite the efforts to create a familiar context, teachers sometimes found the descriptions incomplete. In particular, some teachers indicated that they adapted their instruction to the abilities of their students, and that lack of information about ability levels made it difficult for them to respond to some of the options. Finally, teachers interpreted some nonreform options to be more indicative of reform-oriented teaching than we had anticipated. As will be discussed in Chapter Four, these types of unintended interpretations can affect our modeling results.

In spite of these difficulties, it is important to keep in mind that the vast majority of the responses indicate that the items functioned as anticipated. Teachers' responses suggest that the vignettes were engaging, relevant, and meaningful, and that the vignettes could accurately describe a wide variety of teaching styles. Overall, teachers' understanding of the vignettes was generally similar to our own, but there were also a few areas in which the vignettes could be improved. Additional insights gained from the cognitive interviews can be found in Le et al. (2006).

# CHAPTER FOUR

# Relationships Between Reform-Oriented Instruction and Student Achievement in Mathematics and Science

This chapter presents the results of our analyses of the relationships between student achievement and teacher-level variables. Although the primary focus of the analysis is on instructional practices, we were also interested in understanding other factors that might be related to students' test performance. Thus, we explore the relationships between achievement and curriculum coverage, teacher-background characteristics, and classroom contextual factors.

The first step in the analyses was to investigate to what extent differences in student achievement could be associated with teacher-level variables. Next, we describe the longitudinal modeling procedures we used to investigate the association between student achievement and continued exposure to instructional practice over a three-year period. We then present the results of the main analyses and the findings from teacher interviews that provide additional insight into the relationships between instructional practices and achievement. We conclude with a discussion of model limitations.

## Variance in Student-Achievement Scores

As a first step in investigating the relationship between instructional practice and achievement, we examined how much of the differences in student achievement could possibly be associated with differences among teachers. Mathematically, we can separate and compare the differences ("variation") in student scores within a given teacher's class and the differences (variation) in scores between different teachers' classes. The latter provides an upper bound on the size of any overall effects that might be due to the instructional practices we measured. The logic is as follows: If one teacher's students perform better on average than another teacher's students, the differences in performance could conceivably be due to different actions on the part of the teachers (i.e., these differences in scores might be attributed to teachers). In contrast, if some students do better than others in the same class, those differences in student scores cannot be directly associated with teacher practices or characteristics because the students had the same teacher.[1]

In fact, it is possible (and advantageous) to divide the differences in student scores even further. Variation between students in the same class may well be due to factors such as the student's performance in the prior year or the student's background characteristics (e.g., their socioeconomic status). We can separate out those differences among students in the same class that are accounted for by the student's background and prior status, and those differences that are not. The same can be done with differences in scores that occur between students who have different teachers; we can average the student information (prior scores, background) for each teacher and calculate the extent to which differences between teachers can be accounted for by the aggregate student characteristics of classrooms.

In formal terms, the total variation in student test scores is divided (decomposed) into parts reflecting the proportion of variance among students assigned to the same teacher (within-teacher component) and the proportion between students assigned to different teachers (between-teacher component). Each of these components is further divided into the proportion associated with student prior scores and background and the proportion not explained by anything we know about the students. Figure 4.1 provides this variance decomposition

---

[1] Teacher practices could also affect student achievement indirectly. For example, some teacher practices could have different effects on different kinds of students, even in the same classroom. Thus, a portion of within-classroom variance in student scores could be indirectly accounted for by teacher practice. Later in this monograph (see Appendix 4-C), we discuss models that investigate a number of possible teacher-student interactions of this kind.

for each year, cohort, and achievement measure.[2] The relative length of a component bar represents the percentage of variance in student test scores associated with each of the four components. The first and second bars represent variance between students assigned to the same teacher (within-teacher variance). The bar on the far left represents the variance in student achievement that is explained by student-level predictors—specifically, demographic characteristics and achievement in the year prior to the study (year 0). The second bar from the left represents within-teacher variance not explained by student background. The third and fourth bars reflect the variance between students assigned to different teachers (between-teacher variance). The third bar represents the percentage of variance explained by aggregating student-background characteristics up to the teacher level (e.g., the percentage of minority students in the class, or the average year 0 achievement of the class). Finally, the bar on the far right is the variance among teachers that is not explained by aggregates of student background.

The findings depicted in Figure 4.1 are generally consistent across cohorts, grades, and outcome measures and indicate that student-level differences, not teacher-level differences, explain the largest proportion of the variance in test scores. On average, the proportion of variance within teachers (the sum of the two bars on the left) is about twice as large as the proportion between teachers (the sum of the two bars on the right). The percentage of achievement variance that can be explained by student demographic variables and prior achievement (the sum of the first and third bars) generally remains stable as students move to higher grades. That is, a sizable portion of achievement is related to student background and/or schooling prior to the study, and this relationship does not diminish over the course of the study.

The sum of the two bars on the right can be thought of as an upper bound for the proportion of variance in student achievement that could potentially be explained by instructional practice and other

---

[2] Results for the open-ended outcomes are missing for some years because those tests were not administered in all years.

**Figure 4.1**
**Variance Decomposition of Achievement Scores for Each Year, Cohort, and Outcome**

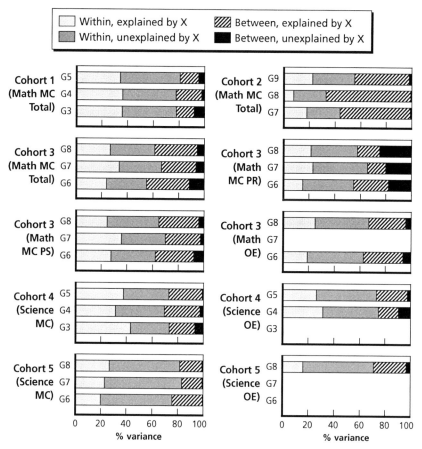

NOTE: For each frame, the four bars from left to right represent percentages of variance explained by within-teacher variation of student demographics and prior scores, unexplained variance within teachers, between-teacher variation explained by teacher-level aggregates of student demographics and prior scores, and unexplained variance between teachers. For Cohorts 1 and 2, only mathematics total MC scores were available. For Cohort 3, these total scores were available, as were the Procedures (PR) and Problem Solving (PS) subscale scores of the MC examination and total scores from the OE examination. For Cohorts 4 and 5, science scores were available for both MC and OE examinations.

classroom- and teacher-level predictors. Furthermore, most of the between-teacher variance is associated with student composition (i.e., generally larger than the fourth). The fourth bar, representing the percentage of variance that is between teachers and not explained by student composition, is generally small, averaging just over 6 percent across all cohorts, outcomes, and years (the average is just over 4 percent if the Cohort 3 PR scores are excluded). This small size implies that a teacher-level variable that explained more than a small percentage of the variance of student achievement would have to be related to student composition—e.g., some practices were used in classes with previously lower-performing students and other practices were used in classes with previously higher-performing students. If this is the case, it is more difficult to isolate the teacher effect statistically. In fact, our measured teacher-level variables were generally not strongly related to the student-composition variables. Collectively, these variance decompositions suggest that the measured teacher-level variables are not likely to explain a large fraction of the variation in student achievement in these data.

## A Statistical Model to Examine the Relationships Between Student Achievement, Reform Instruction, and Other Factors

The primary reason for conducting a study that follows students longitudinally through different teachers is to estimate the cumulative effects on achievement of continued exposure to reform-oriented teaching practices. It is reasonable to assume that achievement in any given year can be explained by a complex mixture of the history of exposure to teaching practices and measured and unmeasured factors relating to individual students and the teachers to whom they are linked. It is conceptually and practically challenging to account for these factors so that inferences can be made about the cumulative effects of exposure to teaching practices.

In this section, we discuss our approach to modeling the relationship between teaching practices and student achievement, and we describe how we dealt with some of the challenges presented by the data and the model.

The first challenge derives from this not being an experimental study with students assigned to particular teachers in particular years. We had to rely on the naturally occurring variation in the assignments of students to teachers to yield students with different exposure to reform-oriented practices. Ideally, we would have controlled the assignment of students to teachers to create sizable groups of students who received sustained high or low exposure to specific teaching practices. Instead, we had to rely on the exposure sequences (i.e., patterns of students' exposure to reform-oriented teaching) that occurred naturally during the study.

As a result, relatively few students in our sample actually received sustained high or sustained low exposure to specific teaching practices. We calculated the percentage of students who consistently received either above-median or below-median exposure to each teacher-level variable for all three years of the study.[3] On average, approximately one-quarter of the students met this criterion (percentages by cohort and teacher-level variable are provided in Appendix 4-A). Similar results were obtained when we looked at groups that experienced more-extreme exposure. We examined the percentage of students consistently receiving either above the 75th-percentile or below the 25th-percentile exposure by grade for all three years. On average, only about 6 percent of students were in high- and low-exposure groups when this more restrictive criterion was used (percentages by cohort and teacher-level variable are provided in Appendix 4-B). Thus, very few students received sustained high exposure or sustained low exposure to practices over three years. The actual percentages are roughly equivalent to what would be obtained if students were assigned at random each year to different levels of reform exposure. This means that few of the students

---

[3] This finding was for those students within each cohort who could be linked to participating teachers across all three years.

in the study had consistently high or consistently low exposure to specific practices, making it more difficult to find associations between cumulative exposure and achievement.

## Model

The modeling approach that we used is a generalization of the model for single-year exposure to teaching practices used in the previous RAND Mosaic I study (Hamilton et al., 2003). In that study, students were linked to teachers (and teaching practices) for a single year. Regression analysis was used to measure the strength of the relationship between teaching practices and student test scores while controlling for differences in student characteristics. Specifically, the effects of single-year exposure were assessed by regressing achievement outcomes on the measures of exposure for that year, adjusting for student-background characteristics and prior achievement.

In the current study, we need to model three years of student-achievement outcomes against three years of exposure to specific teaching practices. To examine the effects of cumulative exposure to teaching practices, achievement outcomes from a given year must be related to both current and past measures of exposure. This condition led us to adopt three parallel regression models. The data from the first year are structurally similar to those from the Mosaic I study, so our regression model for year 1 achievement outcomes is identical to that model. Our models for the achievement outcomes in years 2 and 3 build on this same basic structure, but they extend it to account for past exposures as well as current exposure. So, for example, our model for year 3 regresses student achievement not only on the measures of exposure to teaching practices in year 3 but also on the measures of exposure from years 1 and 2 (as well as student-background characteristics and year 0 achievement).[4] Model details are found in Appendix 4-C.

---

[4] We assume an additive structure for the cumulative effect of exposure, so that, for example, the achievement outcome in year 2 depends on an effect of exposure in year 1 and on an additional additive effect of exposure in year 2. More-complex model equations that relax the additivity assumption, discussed in this chapter, did not lead to substantive changes in the results.

Under the model, exposure to a teacher-level variable in a given year has an effect on student achievement that year, as well as in later years. These effects are allowed to be different, so the model allows us to assess the extent to which the effect of current exposure is transient or persistent into future years. This flexibility of the model motivated us to consider two different types of inferences regarding the effects of teacher practices. The first, which we call the "single-year effect" or "current-year effect," captures the average effect of exposure in a given year on the achievement outcome from that same year. The second effect, which we call the "cumulative effect," captures the total effect on year 3 achievement outcomes of the history of exposure measured during the course of the study. It is estimated by summing the effects of year 1, year 2, and year 3 exposures on year 3 outcomes.

In the current study, we assess the effect of teacher-level variables (including instructional practices) one at a time. That is, we start with a baseline model that includes adjustments for student demographics and year 0 achievement, then examine the effects of a given individual teacher-level variable by adding to the baseline model the particular teacher-level variable under consideration. We conducted these analyses one at a time, because the number of distinct teacher-level variables exceeds 30 and the number of responding teachers averages only about 60 per year per cohort; therefore, it is infeasible to simultaneously model and isolate the partial effects of each variable. Lacking a theoretical justification for selecting a small subset of variables to include in a simultaneous model, we opted to examine each teacher-level variable individually. However, the statistical model we used can be extended to include multiple teacher-level variables simultaneously. For the teaching-practice variables, which are the primary focus of the study, we considered several sensitivity analyses that examined the effects of controlling for other teacher characteristics and classroom contextual variables, described in Appendix 4-D.

## Implementation Issues

We faced two primary challenges in implementing the model. The first challenge stems from having repeated measures taken on students as they progress through different grades and teachers, which leads to a potentially complex set of relationships among the unexplained variance (i.e., residual-error terms) in the regression model that can lead to inefficient estimates of effects and invalid standard errors for such estimates. The problem arises because the residuals are likely to be correlated within students over time and among students who share the same teachers. It is necessary to properly specify these correlations to produce efficient estimates of the effects of interest and, more important, to obtain valid standard errors of these estimates. A popular approach for accounting for nested data structures (i.e., students who share the same teachers) in educational research is multilevel, or hierarchical, linear modeling (HLM; Raudenbush and Bryk, 2002). However, because students change teachers over time, traditional HLM methods designed for analyzing simple hierarchical structures that assume that a student has only one teacher are not appropriate. Rather, specialized methods for cross-classified relational structures (Raudenbush and Bryk, 2002) are required. Thus, we estimated our regression models using the general multivariate linear mixed model presented by McCaffrey et al. (2004). Because the model is complex to estimate using traditional maximum likelihood methods, we used the Bayesian implementation of the model presented by Lockwood, McCaffrey, Mariano, and Setodji (in press), which provides a computationally efficient framework for this class of models. Additional details are provided in Appendix 4-C.

The second challenge to implementing the model was missing data. Across cohorts, the proportion of students with complete data and teacher links for all three years ranged from 10 to 20 percent. We thus developed a multistage multiple imputation process for dealing with missing student and teacher variables and missing student-teacher links. We describe this process in detail in Appendix 4-E. All models presented here were fit separately to each imputed data set, and the overall inferences are based on aggregating results across data sets, using standard multiple-imputation inference procedures (Schafer, 1997).

## Relationships Between Teacher-Level Variables and Student Achievement

For the sake of clarity, we present the findings for mathematics and science separately. In each case, we discuss the single-year and cumulative associations between achievement and instructional practices first, followed by teacher background, curriculum coverage, and classroom context.

Inferences are reported in terms of standardized effect sizes. All continuous variables in the models, including student scores, Instructional Practice scales, and other teacher-level variables were standardized to have mean 0 and variance 1 within each cohort.[5] Thus, the single-year or current-year coefficients represent the expected difference in test-score standard deviations for a one-standard-deviation unit increase in the teacher-level variable. Similarly, the three-year cumulative exposure effect can be interpreted as the expected difference in year 3 standardized scores between two students, one of whom received one-standard-deviation-above-average exposure to the particular practice under consideration for three consecutive years and the other of whom received exactly average exposure for three consecutive years.

Statistical significance was assessed by adjusting our nearly 500 statistical tests (different teacher-level variables, different cohort-outcome combinations, and current-year versus cumulative effects) for multiple comparisons using a false discovery rate procedure (Benjamini and Hochberg, 1995). A false discovery rate is the proportion of predictions that can be expected to be reported as showing significant relationships when no relationships actually exist. Applying the procedure led to rejecting the null hypothesis of zero effect when $p$-values are less than .03. This standard was applied to all the models examining the relationship among variables for student achievement and instructional

---

[5] The standardization to unit variance in each year did not distort any key features of the data, because the marginal variance of the original scaled scores was approximately constant across years. The dichotomous teacher-level predictors (e.g., master's degree, math degree, heterogeneous classroom) were not transformed.

practices, teacher characteristics, curriculum coverage, and classroom context (i.e., Figures 4.2 through 4.5). Additional details are provided in Appendix 4-F.

### Mathematics Results

As noted, the longitudinal framework employed for the study allowed us to estimate the relationships between achievement and instructional practice, both for single years and cumulatively across time. Figure 4.2 presents graphical representations of the relationships between mathematics achievement and single-year exposure to reform-oriented teaching, teacher-background characteristics, curriculum coverage, and classroom context. Figure 4.3 presents analogous results for cumulative exposure. The gray dots represent positive relationships with achievement, and the black dots indicate negative relationships. The magnitude of the relationships is indicated by the area of the dot: The larger dots represent stronger relationships, and the smaller dots represent weaker relationships (statistically significant results are indicated with an asterisk). Appendixes 4-G and 4-H provide the standardized coefficients for each scale within each cohort for the single-year and cumulative exposure analyses, respectively.

**Instructional Practices Show Mostly Nonsignificant Relationships with Mathematics Achievement.** An important purpose of this study was to investigate whether weak, short-term relationships between reform teaching and student achievement can cumulate into stronger relationships if the reforms were sustained. There is some evidence that the effects of reform teaching on achievement are larger with prolonged exposure. The relationships between instructional practices and student achievement are generally in the same direction for single-year exposure (Figure 4.2) as for cumulative exposure (Figure 4.3), but the relationships become stronger as students and teachers are involved in

**Figure 4.2**
**Relationships Between Variables for Instructional Practices, Curriculum Coverage, Teacher Background, and Classroom Context and Mathematics Achievement (Single-Year Exposure)**

Legend: ● –0.15   ● –0.1   • –0.05   ○ 0.05   ◯ 0.1   ◯ 0.15

| | | Cohort 1 Grades 3–5 MC TO | Cohort 2 Grades 7–9 MC TO | Cohort 3 Grades 6–8 MC TO | Cohort 3 Grades 6–8 MC PR | Cohort 3 Grades 6–8 MC PS | Cohort 3 Grades 6–8 OE |
|---|---|---|---|---|---|---|---|
| Instructional Practices | Reform-High | ○ | ∘ | ○ | ○ | ∘ | ○ |
| | Reform-Full | ∘ | ● | ● | ●* | ○ | ○ |
| | Reform Practices | ● | ∘ | ∘ | ● | ○ | ○ |
| | Reform Relative to Text | ∘ | ○ | ∘ | ● | ○ | ○ |
| | Mathematical Processes | ○* | ∘ | ● | ● | • | ○ |
| | Hours Weekly Instruction | ○ | ○* | ● | ●* | • | ● |
| | Discussion | ∘ | ∘ | ● | ●* | • | ○ |
| | Groupwork | ●* | ● | • | ● | ○ | ○* |
| | Mixed-Ability Groupwork | ●* | ● | ● | ●* | ○ | ○* |
| | Problem-Solving Groupwork | ●* | ● | ● | ●* | ○ | ○* |
| | Average Reform Activities | ○* | • | ○ | ● | ○ | ○ |
| | Time On Task | ○ | ○ | ○ | • | ○* | ○ |
| | Seatwork | ○* | ● | • | ●* | ○ | ○ |
| Curriculum Coverage | Operations | ∘ | ● | ∘ | ● | ○ | ○ |
| | Algebra | ○ | ● | • | ● | ○ | ◯ |
| Teacher Background | Professional Development | ○ | • | ○ | ○ | • | ∘ |
| | Experience | ○* | ○* | ○ | ∘ | ○* | ○* |
| | Experience at Grade | ○ | ○* | ○ | ○ | ○* | ○* |
| | Master's Degree | ○ | ○* | ○ | ● | ○* | ∘ |
| | Math Degree | — | ○ | ●* | ●* | ●* | ●* |
| | Confidence | ○ | ○ | • | ○ | ● | ∘ |
| Class Context | Heterogeneous Classroom | ● | ● | ● | ●* | ○ | ○ |
| | Class Size | ○ | ○* | ● | ●* | ○ | ○ |

*Indicates statistical significance.
NOTES: MC TO = Total Multiple-Choice score; MC PR = Mathematics Procedure subscale score; MC PS = Mathematics Problem-Solving subscale score; OE = Total Open-Ended Score. Mathematical Processes, Average Reform Activities, Hours Weekly Instruction, and Algebra were available for years 2 and 3 only.

**Figure 4.3**
**Relationships Between Variables for Instructional Practices, Curriculum Coverage, Teacher Background, and Classroom Context and Mathematics Achievement (Cumulative Exposure)**

| ● −0.15 | ● −0.1 | ● −0.05 | ○ 0.05 | ○ 0.1 | ○ 0.15 |

|  |  | Cohort 1 Grades 3–5 MC TO | Cohort 2 Grades 7–9 MC TO | Cohort 3 Grades 6–8 MC TO | Cohort 3 Grades 6–8 MC PR | Cohort 3 Grades 6–8 MC PS | Cohort 3 Grades 6–8 OE |
|---|---|---|---|---|---|---|---|
| **Instructional Practices** | Reform-High | ○ | ○ | • | ○ | ● | ● |
|  | Reform-Full | ∘ | ∘ | ○ | • | ○ * | ○ |
|  | Reform Practices | ○ | • | ○ |  | ○ | ○ |
|  | Reform Relative to Text | ○ | ○ | ○ | ● | ○ | ○ |
|  | Mathematical Processes | ○ | ○ | ● | ● * |  | ○ |
|  | Hours Weekly Instruction | ○ | ○ | ● | ● * | ∘ | ○ |
|  | Discussion | ○ | ○ | ∘ | ● | ○ | ○ |
|  | Groupwork | ● | ● * | ● | ● | ∘ | ○ * |
|  | Mixed-Ability Groupwork | ● | ● * | ● | ● * | ○ | ○ * |
|  | Problem-Solving Groupwork | ● | ● | ● | ● * | ○ | ○ * |
|  | Average Reform Activities | ○ |  | ○ * | ○ * | ○ | ○ |
|  | Time On Task | ○ | ○ | ○ | ○ | ○ * | ○ |
|  | Seatwork | ○ * | ● | ● | ● * | ● | ○ |
| **Curriculum Coverage** | Operations | ● | ● | ○ | ○ | ● | ○ |
|  | Algebra | ○ | ● | ∘ | ○ | ∘ | ○ |
| **Teacher Background** | Professional Development | ● | ● | ○ | ○ | ● | ● |
|  | Experience | ∘ | ○ * | ○ | ○ | ○ * | ○ * |
|  | Experience at Grade | ● | ○ * | ∘ |  | ○ | ○ |
|  | Master's Degree | ○ | ○ * | ● | ● * | ○ | ● |
|  | Math Degree | — | ○ | ● | ● * | ● * | ○ |
|  | Confidence | ∘ | ○ * | • | ○ | ○ |  |
| **Class Context** | Heterogeneous Classroom | ● | ● * | ● | ● * | ○ | • |
|  | Class Size | ○ | ○ * | ○ * | ∘ | ○ * | ○ |

*Indicates statistical significance.
NOTES: MC TO = Total Multiple-Choice score; MC PR = Mathematics Procedure subscale score; MC PS = Mathematics Problem-Solving subscale score; OE = Total Open-Ended Score. Mathematical Processes, Average Reform Activities, Hours Weekly Instruction, and Algebra were available for years 2 and 3 only.

RAND MG480-4.3

the reform for longer periods of time.[6] Formal tests of whether cumulative effects are detectably different from current-year effects (not shown) indicated that when the two effects differ markedly, that difference is generally statistically significant.

In both figures, the relationships between mathematics achievement and reform-oriented practice are mostly nonsignificant, including relationships that involve the more-innovative vignette-based measures.[7] Although the relationships are not statistically significant, the majority of the reform-oriented practices are positively signed with total MC performance after three years of cumulative exposure. The exception to the trend that reform-oriented teaching is positively signed with total MC achievement involves groupwork-related activities. Groupwork-related practices show a consistent negative relationship with total MC achievement. In Cohort 1, single-year exposure to groupwork, to groupwork involving students of mixed ability, and to groupwork involving collaboration to solve new problems is significantly and negatively associated with MC scores. In Cohort 2, sustained exposure to groupwork and to mixed-ability groupwork is also significantly negatively related with MC performance. Similar patterns are observed with respect to cumulative exposure for Cohort 3, although the relationships are not significant.

**Conclusions About the Effectiveness of Reform-Oriented Instruction May Depend on How Mathematics Achievement Is Measured.** As noted earlier, there are significant negative relationships between groupwork-related practices and total MC scores in Cohorts 1 and 2, and suggestive negative associations in Cohort 3. In contrast, there are

---

[6] Although the relationships between instructional practice and student achievement are weaker for single-year exposure than for cumulative exposure, the instructional-practice variables were more likely to reach statistical significance under the former analysis. This trend is due to the larger standard errors associated with the cumulative-year effects, which involve the sum of three unknown parameters. In contrast, the current-year parameters involve an average of three unknown parameters (i.e., average of year 1 effects on year 1 outcomes, year 2 effects on year 2 outcomes, and year 3 effects on year 3 outcomes), and averaging reduces the standard error.

[7] In Figures 4.2 and 4.3, most of the instructional-practices variables are considered reform-oriented. The exceptions are Hours of Weekly Instruction, Time on Task, and Seatwork.

significant positive relationships between groupwork-related practices and OE scores in Cohort 3. This finding provides suggestive evidence that the relationship between reform practice and achievement can be influenced by the manner in which achievement is measured. The result also raises questions about whether the MC and OE tests measure different constructs. Many advocates of reform-oriented teaching believe that traditional MC tests do not adequately reflect the range of competencies the reforms are expected to develop, and tests requiring students to construct their answers and to engage in complex problem solving are more appropriate.

Additional evidence about potentially different relationships between instructional practices and measures of achievement comes from examining PR and PS scores in mathematics. Instructional practices that are significantly related to one type of achievement measure showed no association or the opposite relationship with the other outcome measure. This dichotomy is best exemplified by Reform-Full, which is a measure of teachers' propensity to engage in reform-oriented instruction. Students whose teachers reported greater inclinations toward using reform-oriented strategies demonstrated poorer single-year PR performance than did students whose teachers were less likely to engage in reform practices. However, when PS scores are the outcome measure, significant positive relationships are observed; students whose teachers are more partial to engaging in reform teaching demonstrate superior cumulative PS performance. In a similar manner, students whose teachers reported more discussion of students' thinking and more groupwork-related activities showed significantly worse PR performance (in the single-year or cumulative analysis), but these same instructional activities are unrelated to students' PS performance.

We conducted additional analysis to calculate the difference in standard-deviation units between each student's score on the PS items and his or her score on the PR items, and we modeled these differences as a function of instructional practices and student-background characteristics (analogous to the approach used by Hamilton et al., 2003). This analysis allowed us to formally test whether there are differences in the effectiveness of reform-oriented teaching on PS relative to PR. We observed significant differences for practices relating to mixed-ability groupwork and groupwork involving collaboration to solve new problems. In both cases, the significant differences stemmed from the groupwork-related practices having positive relationships with PS and negative relationships with PR.

Although not significant, other reform-oriented instructional practices also tend to be positively signed with PS scores and negatively signed with PR scores—a pattern that suggests that reform-oriented teaching may enhance higher-order thinking skills and that also raises questions about the apparent trade-off between PS and PR improvements. Theoretically, reform-oriented teaching is believed to promote the kinds of skills that are measured by both the PR and PS subscales (NCTM, 1989; 2000). That we observe negative relationships with PR (some of which reach statistical significance) may suggest that teachers had trouble fully implementing the reform in a manner that reflects the principles envisioned by its advocates. Indeed, many studies have found that teachers perceive themselves to be engaging in reform-oriented activities, whereas observers judge their teaching to be indicative of nonreform pedagogy (Cohen, 1990; Ingle and Cory, 1999; Mayer, 1999). The extent to which the effectiveness of reform-oriented teaching depends on the proportion of PR or PS items included on a given measure of mathematics achievement merits further investigation, as does the role of teachers' implementation of certain instructional approaches.

**Relationships Between Instruction and Mathematics Achievement Vary by Grade Level and Cohort.** Relationships between instructional strategies and achievement are not always consistent across different grade levels or cohorts. Seatwork, for example, is positively related to total MC scores in the elementary grades (i.e., Cohort 1), but it is unrelated (with some evidence of negative relationships) to total MC achievement at the middle grades (i.e., Cohorts 2 and 3). Given that the samples in Cohort 1 and Cohort 2 consisted of students in the same district but in different grades, the differences in relationships are likely to be due, in part, to differences in the effectiveness of the practices with different age groups.

Similarly, measures of the amount of mathematics instruction show different relationships to mathematics achievement, depending on the cohort in question. In Cohort 2, the amount of weekly mathematics instruction reported by teachers is positively related to mathematics achievement; in Cohort 3, however, there is a negative relationship. This anomalous finding may reflect a concerted effort by teachers to provide longer or more-intensive mathematics instruction to students who are in the most need of mathematics improvement.

**Four Teacher Characteristics Are Related to Higher Mathematics Achievement.** Four teacher-background measures show fairly consistent relationships with achievement. Total teaching experience is positively associated with MC performance in the elementary grades. At the middle grades, teaching experience, both in total and at grade level, is associated with higher test scores, as is holding a master's degree. Somewhat unexpectedly, having a middle school teacher with an undergraduate mathematics degree was negatively related to student mathematics performance in the current year, regardless of the type of outcome measure. This unanticipated finding merits more research, but it may reflect purposive assignment practices by districts or schools to place more-qualified teachers in the classrooms of more-challenging students.

**Curriculum Coverage and Classroom Contextual Factors Are Mostly Unrelated to Mathematics Achievement.** Coverage of operations and algebraic topics is not related to mathematics achievement at the elementary or middle grades, regardless of achievement outcome measure. The lack of strong relationships is likely to be due in part to the content of the tests, which assess other areas of mathematics (e.g., geometry) that are not included in the Operations or Algebra scales.

Additionally, large class size is positively associated with mathematics achievement, and heterogeneity in students' mathematics abilities was negatively related to student performance. These two latter findings may be related to tracking policies that typically occur during the middle grade years. It is possible that lower-achieving students were assigned to smaller classrooms to allow for individualized attention and that higher-achieving students were assigned to classrooms of peers with similar abilities. These types of tracking practices would result in the patterns that we observed. However, we did not investigate whether tracking policies were implemented in these particular schools or districts.

## Science Results

Figures 4.4 and 4.5 present the results of single-year and cumulative analyses for student science achievement (see Appendixes 4-G and 4-H for the single-year and cumulative coefficients, respectively). As in mathematics, there is a tendency for the cumulative effects to be larger than the current-year effects. Additionally, relationships in science are generally stronger than those observed for mathematics.

**Relationships Between Reform-Oriented Practices and Science Achievement Are Nonsignificant or Weakly Positive.** Although the majority of the reform-oriented practices show nonsignificant relationships to total MC scores, most are positively signed. The few reform-oriented practices that reach statistical significance relate to discussion of students' thinking, frequency of selected reform practices (such as use of extended investigations), hands-on science, and groupwork-related activities. The finding regarding groupwork differs from that observed in mathematics, for which groupwork-related practices are negatively associated with student performance on MC items.

Stronger relationships are also observed with OE scores than with MC scores. Across both cohorts, reform-oriented practices relating to emphasis on experiments, problem solving in groups, mixed-ability groupwork, and hands-on activities are positively, albeit weakly, associated with OE measures of achievement, as is intention to engage in reform teaching (i.e., Reform-Full). These same strategies show nonsignificant relationships to MC performance—again suggesting that inferences about the effectiveness of reform teaching may depend on how achievement is measured.

**Relationships Between Instructional Practices and Student Science Achievement Vary by Grade.** There are grade-specific differences in the strength of relationships: The associations between

**Figure 4.4**
**Relationships Between Variables for Instructional Practices, Curriculum Coverage, Teacher Background, and Classroom Context and Science Achievement (Single-Year Exposure)**

Legend: ● –0.15   ● –0.1   • –0.05   ○ 0.05   ○ 0.1   ◯ 0.15

| | | Cohort 4 Grades 3–5 MC | Cohort 4 Grades 3–5 OE | Cohort 5 Grades 6–8 MC | Cohort 5 Grades 6–8 OE |
|---|---|---|---|---|---|
| **Instructional Practices** | Reform-High | ○ | ○ | ○ | ○ |
| | Reform-Full | ○ | ○* | ○ | ○ |
| | Reform Practices | ○ | ○ | ○* | ○* |
| | Experiments | ○ | ○ | ○ | ○* |
| | Hours Weekly Instruction | ● | ○ | ○ | ○ |
| | Discussion | ○* | ● | ○ | ● |
| | Groupwork | ● | ○ | ○ | ○ |
| | Mixed-Ability Groupwork | ● | ○ | ○* | ○ |
| | Problem-Solving Groupwork | ● | ○ | ○* | ○ |
| | Average Reform Activities | ○ | ○ | ○ | ○* |
| | Time On Task | ○ | ○ | ● | ○ |
| | Hands-On | ● | ○ | ○* | ○ |
| | Seatwork | ○ | ● | ● | • |
| **Curriculum Coverage** | Earth Science | | ○* | — | — |
| | Life Science | ○ | ○* | — | — |
| | Physical Science | • | ○ | — | — |
| | Reasoning and Technology | ○ | ○ | — | — |
| | Science Content | ○ | ○* | ○ | ○ |
| | Kits | ○ | ○ | — | — |
| | Sleuths | — | — | ○ | ○ |
| **Teacher Background** | Professional Development | ● | ○ | ○ | ○ |
| | Experience | ○ | ○* | ○ | ● |
| | Experience at Grade | ○ | ○* | ○* | |
| | Science Degree | — | — | ○* | ◯ |
| | Master's Degree | ○ | ◯ | ○ | ● |
| | Confidence | ○ | ○ | ○ | ◯ |
| **Class Context** | Heterogeneous Classroom | ◯ | ◯ | ○ | ◯ |
| | Class Size | ○ | ● | • | ● |
| | Materials Availability | — | — | ○* | ○* |

*Indicates statistical significance.
NOTES: MC = Total Multiple-Choice score; OE = Total Open-Ended score.
Average Reform Activities and Hours Weekly Instruction were available for years 2 and 3 only.

**Figure 4.5**
**Relationships Between Variables for Instructional Practices, Curriculum Coverage, Teacher Background, and Classroom Context and Science Achievement (Cumulative Exposure)**

Legend: ● −0.15　● −0.1　• −0.05　○ 0.05　◯ 0.1　◯ 0.15

| | | Cohort 4 Grades 3–5 MC | Cohort 4 Grades 3–5 OE | Cohort 5 Grades 6–8 MC | Cohort 5 Grades 6–8 OE |
|---|---|:---:|:---:|:---:|:---:|
| **Instructional Practices** | Reform-High | • | ○ | ◯ | ○ |
| | Reform-Full | ○ | ◯ * | ° | ◯ * |
| | Reform Practices | ● | • | ◯ * | ◯ * |
| | Experiments | ° | ◯ * | ○ | ◯ * |
| | Hours Weekly Instruction | ● | • | ○ | ◯ |
| | Discussion | ● | ○ | • | ○ |
| | Groupwork | ○ | ◯ * | ○ | ◯ |
| | Mixed-Ability Groupwork | ○ | ◯ * | ○ | ◯ * |
| | Problem-Solving Groupwork | ○ | ◯ | ◯ * | ◯ * |
| | Average Reform Activities | • | ° | ○ | ◯ |
| | Time On Task | ○ | ◯ | ● | ○ |
| | Hands-On | ○ | ◯ * | ◯ * | ◯ * |
| | Seatwork | ○ | ● * | ● | ○ |
| **Curriculum Coverage** | Earth Science | ○ | ◯ | — | — |
| | Life Science | ○ | ◯ * | — | — |
| | Physical Science | ○ | ◯ | — | — |
| | Reasoning and Technology | ° | ◯ | — | — |
| | Science Content | ○ | ◯ | ○ | ◯ * |
| | Kits | • | ◯ * | — | — |
| | Sleuths | — | — | ◯ | ◯ |
| **Teacher Background** | Professional Development | ● | • | ° | ○ |
| | Experience | ○ * | ◯ * | ○ | ° |
| | Experience at Grade | ○ * | ◯ * | ○ * | ○ |
| | Science Degree | — | — | ◯ * | ◯ |
| | Master's Degree | ◯ | ◯ * | ° | ° |
| | Confidence | ◯ * | ◯ | ◯ * | ◯ |
| **Class Context** | Heterogeneous Classroom | ○ | ◯ | ● | ◯ |
| | Class Size | ○ | ◯ | ○ | • |
| | Materials Availability | — | — | ◯ * | ◯ * |

*Indicates statistical significance.
NOTES: MC = Total Multiple-Choice score; OE = Total Open-Ended score.
Average Reform Activities and Hours Weekly Instruction were available for years 2 and 3 only.

reform-oriented teaching and achievement are generally stronger in the middle grades (Cohort 5) than in the elementary grades (Cohort 4). In the elementary-grades cohort, single-year exposure to discussion of students' thinking is positively related to MC score. In the middle school cohort, single-year and cumulative exposure to Hands-On, Problem-Solving Groupwork, and Reform Practices are associated with improved MC performance. It is unclear to what extent these cohort-specific relationships are due to differences in grade levels as opposed to differences in district policies, but they suggest that the effectiveness of specific reform-oriented practices may depend on the ages of the students.

**Few Teacher Background and Classroom Context Variables Are Related to Science Achievement.** Two teacher-background variables show consistent patterns with student outcomes. In both cohorts, students with teachers who had more experience teaching at grade level and more confidence in their science knowledge outscore their peers, whose teachers had less experience and were not as confident in their science knowledge. Additionally, in Cohort 4, having more teaching experience and having a master's degree are positively associated with test scores; in Cohort 5, having a science degree is associated with higher science achievement. The two latter findings regarding a master's degree (Ferguson and Ladd, 1996) and science-specific undergraduate degree (Goldhaber and Brewer, 2000) are consistent with those of other studies.

Of the classroom-context variables, only the Materials Availability scale is significantly associated with test scores. Greater access to science tools is associated with better MC and OE performance. Again, this finding is likely a reflection of opportunity to learn, whereby students who have greater access to equipment and resources have more opportunities to participate in activities that foster scientific understanding.

**Greater Coverage of Curriculum Predicts Science Achievement.** In the elementary-grade cohort, greater coverage of life science and earth science is associated with higher achievement on OE measures. This is not surprising, given that the SAT-9 OE tasks draw from life, earth, and physical sciences (Harcourt Assessment, 1996a). In the middle school cohort, greater coverage of core science content is also associated with higher OE achievement. This result is consistent with those of other studies that have found that more exposure to science content is associated with higher science achievement (Gamoran et al., 1997; Schmidt and McKnight, 1995), and it may reflect greater opportunities for students to encounter content that is included on the tests.

## Explaining the Empirical Results with Teacher Interviews

During the third and fourth years of the study, we interviewed a total of 60 mathematics and science teachers to gauge their interpretations of reform-oriented teaching and to better understand the factors that facilitate or constrain their implementation of reform-oriented instruction. Teachers' responses shed light on some of the findings of the empirical analyses. The weak relationships between reform-oriented instruction and achievement may be explained by contextual factors that we did not measure—accountability assessments being foremost: Nearly all the mathematics and science teachers we interviewed indicated that the content of their state accountability assessments was not amenable to reform-oriented practices. Needing to cover all the topics that were included in the broad state assessments, both mathematics and science teachers indicated that they shied away from reform-oriented activities that were perceived to be time-consuming, such as student-initiated research or assignments that required work in the computer lab. They also reported increasing the amount of time spent on conventional activities (e.g., assigning worksheets) that they believed would lead to a demonstrable increase in student achievement on the state tests.

Additionally, some teachers noted that, in the face of pressures from accountability provisions attached to the state standardized assessments, they continued to implement reform-oriented practices, but not as fully as they might have. Mathematics teachers, for example, reported that they used manipulatives in their lessons, but they did not allow as much time for students to explore with the manipulatives as they would have in the absence of state accountability tests. Similarly, science teachers indicated that they encouraged dialogue among their students, but they did not foster much in-depth discussion, given the constraints of the number of topics they needed to cover. If such superficial implementation of reform-oriented teaching is widespread, it might help explain the patterns of weak relationships between reform-oriented instruction and achievement. More findings about the various influences on teachers' practices can be found in Chau et al. (2006).

The weak relationships may also stem from teachers' interpretations of the survey items describing different teaching behaviors. Cognitive interviews with teachers indicated that some teachers interpreted nonreform or low-reform options to be more reform-oriented than we had intended. For example, such low-reform options as teachers directing students toward a solution instead of allowing the students to uncover their own mistakes was unexpectedly interpreted by some teachers as characterizing reform-oriented principles. In other instances, teachers interpreted nonreform options that were intended to emphasize procedural learning goals as encompassing broader understanding of the material. Other studies have found that teachers' interpretations of specific behaviors do not always match researchers' understandings (Cohen, 1990; Ingle and Cory, 1999; Mayer, 1999), and these differences could have contributed to the failure to find large effects.

## Model Limitations

Although this study represents a methodological advance over earlier studies, limitations remain that might be contributing to the failure to find large effects and that could be addressed in future research. One of the primary limitations is the study's reliance on naturally occurring variation in exposure to reform-oriented instruction. We did not assign students to teachers in a systematic manner, and relying on natural variation yielded few students who actually received three consecutive years of high-reform (or alternatively, nonreform) instruction. Thus, we had to rely on assumptions about the form of the function (model equation) relating exposure history to achievement to estimate the cumulative effect of sustained exposure to reform instruction. (See Appendix 4-C.) Although our inferences were robust to some extensions to the basic linear, additive model at the core of our analysis, it is still possible that the assumptions underlying the model equations were flawed, leading to biased estimates of the true effect of consistent exposure.

Relying on naturally occurring variation in student-teacher linkages also opens the study to the possibility of selection bias, whereby students with higher achievement or growth potential are linked to teachers more likely to engage in particular practices. The practice of assigning students to teachers or classrooms based on student ability is not uncommon, even in schools that do not implement a formal tracking policy. Although we controlled for all observable student characteristics in our data, including prior achievement, and did not find strong relationships between these characteristics and instructional practices, selection bias cannot be ruled out.

## Summary of Findings

The analyses were designed to address two research questions about the relationships between instructional practice and student achievement. We briefly summarize the findings related to each of these questions.

**What are the relationships between reform-oriented practices and student achievement over a three-year period?** With the exception of groupwork-related practices in mathematics (for which the relationships were negative), reform-oriented instructional practices have nonsignificant relationships with student achievement. However, many of these reform-oriented practices are also positively signed. Specific results vary across grade levels and across subjects, with positive relationships observed more frequently in science than in mathematics. Variation across grades and subjects is not surprising, since the contexts are very different, and we may expect certain practices to be differentially effective in different subjects and/or with students of different ages.

The longitudinal framework employed for the analysis further allowed us to estimate the relationships between achievement and instructional practice, both for single years and cumulatively across time. For variables that appeared to be related to achievement, there was evidence that cumulative effects were stronger than current-year effects.

**Are certain types of achievement measures more sensitive to the effects of reform-oriented practices?** We observed generally stronger reform-oriented relationships for OE measures than for MC measures in the sites at which both types of assessment were administered. Moreover, in the cohort for whom we had data on subscales of the MC mathematics achievement test, we observed stronger relationships for the PS subscale than for the PR subscale.

Together, these findings suggest that interpretations of relationships between instruction and achievement can depend on how achievement is measured. In this case, it is possible that OE tests and PS items are more closely aligned with the skills fostered by the reform-oriented approach than are the MC items, particularly those MC items measuring procedural knowledge. Although the differences between the results obtained with different measures are generally small, they may be large enough to lead to different conclusions about the relationships of reform-oriented practices and student achievement. In particular, reform-oriented instruction may be especially effective in improving skills measured by OE or PS items, and tests that rely solely on MC items or that contain a large proportion of PR items may lead to overly pessimistic interpretations about the efficacy of reform-oriented teaching.

# CHAPTER FIVE

# Implications

The analyses described in this monograph suggest that, over a three-year period, greater exposure to reform-oriented instruction was generally not significantly associated with higher student achievement. Those relatively weak positive associations between reform-oriented instruction and achievement that were found are consistent with the findings of a number of earlier studies.

However, the results reinforce two important messages. The first message is that measurement matters: The choice of achievement measure leads to somewhat different conclusions about the strength of the relationship between achievement and reform-oriented instruction. In particular, achievement measures that appeared to be reasonably well aligned with the goals of the reforms—i.e., open-ended assessments and items that measured problem-solving skills—were most sensitive to the effects of reform-oriented instruction. Unfortunately, most existing state and district tests are not well aligned with reform-oriented approaches, and it is common practice to use existing state or district tests as measures of program effectiveness because the tests have official approval and scores are easy to obtain. This lack of alignment limits the value of state and district tests for judging the effect of such programs, a shortcoming that is not easily addressed because it is often difficult to convince district or school personnel to agree to additional test administration. In today's high-stakes testing environment, there is a widespread perception among educators that testing burdens are already excessive (Pedulla et al., 2003).

The second message is that using subscales from an existing test to produce a more refined analysis of relationships between instruction and achievement can provide important insights. Many standard-ized tests produce subscale scores that differentiate among domains of performance. Although, at present, subscale scores are rarely used in accountability systems, this analysis suggests they should not be overlooked when program effect and student-achievement growth are being investigated. The use of measures that are aligned with the goals of the reform will improve the validity of evaluation findings, and it might also lead to better reform implementation by encouraging teach-ers to focus on these goals. Indeed, in interviews, many teachers cited competing goals as one of the factors leading them to shy away from reform-oriented practices.

## Explaining Weak Relationships

The weak relationships we observed might be attributable, in part, to the analytic limitations of our modeling approach, which we discussed in Chapter Four. An additional possible explanation for the weak relationships is that the instructional-practice measures we used did not adequately measure teachers' use of reform strategies. Despite our efforts to expand the standard repertoire of teacher self-report mea-sures, it is quite likely that we failed to fully capture the ways in which teachers implemented reform-oriented practices in their classrooms.

Perhaps more importantly, the variance decompositions presented in Chapter Four show that a sizable portion of the variation in stu-dent achievement occurred among students sharing the same teacher and could not be explained by anything observable about the students. That is, neither knowing the students' past achievements nor know-ing which teacher taught the students explained how much the stu-dents were likely to grow in achievement. It is possible that some of this unexplained variance is due to differential effectiveness of reform-oriented instruction across students within a classroom. It might also be due to differentiated instruction that we were unable to measure. Such differentiated instruction might stem from teachers forming ability-based groups within class or across different classrooms taught by middle school teachers. It might also involve more-subtle instructional differentiation, as when teachers ask more-difficult questions to higher-achieving students than they do to lower-achieving students.

Such differentiation would not have been picked up by our instructional measures. For example, teachers might have provided accurate reports of average time spent on an activity, such as problem solving, but students within the same classrooms might have experienced different levels of exposure as a result of such factors as student characteristics and effort, grouping, or the specific feedback or questions provided by the teachers (Yoon and Resnick, 1998; Martinez-Fernandez, 2005). Furthermore, the instruction some students receive might be more effective than the instruction other students receive.

If differentiated instruction is common, then valid attempts to measure students' exposure to reform-oriented practices might have to take place at the student level rather than at the teacher level (Gamoran, 1991; Muthen et al., 1995)—for example, through student surveys. However, some earlier research casts doubt on the accuracy of such surveys when specialized terminology and complex instructional practice are involved (see, e.g., Burstein et al., 1995, and Herman, Klein, and Abedi, 2000). Other possible methods include teacher or student logs or observations that examine specific student-teacher interactions (Camburn and Barnes, 2004; Rowan, Camburn, and Correnti, 2004; Rowan, Harrison, and Hayes, 2004).

An additional explanation for the weak relationships comes from our interviews, which suggested that teachers' interpretations of what it means to engage in reform-oriented pedagogy might not match researchers' understanding of such engagement. Descriptions of behaviors that we had intended as reflecting nonreform instruction were interpreted by teachers as embodying reform principles, and these differences could have contributed to the small effects. Many teachers also felt compelled to deviate from the curriculum and instruction emphasized by their local reform initiatives because of the pressures associated with state test–based accountability systems. Teachers reported spending less time on nontested material and activities (e.g., student-initiated research) than they would have in the absence of state accountability tests and more time supplementing their reform-oriented curriculum with worksheets or other activities that they perceived would help ensure that students acquired the skills necessary for success on state tests. Teachers also noted that, because the state standards were so broad and numerous, they did not implement reform-oriented pedagogy as fully as they would have liked. For example, they reported curtailing student exploration and discussion in an attempt to cover topics included on the state standardized tests.

All these actions might have diminished teachers' emphasis on reform-oriented instruction, even among teachers who scored high on our measures of reform orientation. As these teacher comments illustrate, competing priorities can act as constraints on the implementation of instructional reforms, as well as on the importance of understanding the context in which reforms are implemented.

## Implementing Reform-Oriented Instruction: Where to Go from Here

Of course, it is possible that the weak observed relationships accurately reflect the effects of reform practices on achievement. Although most of the existing studies on the effects of instruction, including the study described in this monograph, rely on designs that are not optimal for supporting causal inferences, there is little evidence of strong effects. Taken as a whole, the literature suggests that encouraging teachers to adopt reform-oriented instruction is unlikely to be an effective strategy for promoting large and rapid improvement in students' mathematics and science achievement as measured by widely used tests. Even among studies that have shown positive relationships, the effect sizes have been small, and seemingly contrasting approaches, such as traditional instruction, have also demonstrated positive effects.

At the same time, some teachers who adopt reform-oriented strategies are able to promote improved student learning. Efforts to adopt any new instructional approach should recognize that other factors, such as the skills and training of the teacher, the curriculum that is in place, and the policy context surrounding the reforms, will inevitably influence the degree to which instruction improves achievement.

Instructional reforms are not carried out in a vacuum, and to be effective, these reforms should be carefully coordinated with efforts to improve other aspects of the instructional context. The LSC programs attempted to align many of these contextual factors in the service of improved mathematics and science achievement, but they were only partially successful (Boyd et al., 2003). Future research on the effectiveness of reform-oriented instruction must incorporate the broader contextual factors as well as the specific elements of the intervention.

Our understanding of the effects of reform-oriented instruction could also be improved through different approaches to research. Most of the studies of reform-oriented practice have been conducted in the context of large national programs, such as the LSC program. Consequently, researchers are unable to utilize the most-rigorous designs, including the use of control groups and random assignment. Statistical techniques that adjust for existing differences among students and teachers help to overcome this limitation, but they cannot fully account for unmeasured differences.

A randomized experiment could provide a powerful test of the effect of reform-oriented practices, and it seems to us that an experimental study of these practices would be the next logical step. Experiments are sometimes difficult to implement in practice, and they require securing cooperation from participating districts. But the information they produce would almost certainly justify the effort. Given the importance of contextual factors, as noted above, it would be desirable to conduct this experiment in a variety of school and district contexts.

Another approach that should be undertaken is to examine the costs and benefits of programs to promote reform-oriented practice. The mathematics and science initiatives of the 1990s were relatively expensive (from the perspective of national reforms). In total, systemic reform initiatives promoting reform-oriented instruction have received approximately $100 million per year in NSF funding, and many of these initiatives have been supplemented by corporate donations and grants from private foundations (Klein et al., 2000; Williams, 1998). And although these initiatives appear to have had some effects on mathematics and science teaching, it is impossible to know whether they are cost-effective and should be followed in future reforms. Data should be collected to compare the benefits and costs of different initiatives. Lack of attention to the cost of reforms weakens options when policymakers are confronted with new challenges. A program of research that involved experimental studies with clear delineation of costs would provide a strong foundation for future decisions about educational reforms.

# Appendixes

Chapters Two through Four refer to appendixes that present technical details of the analysis. These appendixes are contained in the CD-ROM attached to the inside back cover of this monograph. They are designated first by the number of the chapter to which they pertain, then by a letter indicating the order in which they are cited in that chapter.

# References

Ajzen, I., and M. Fishbein, *Understanding Attitudes and Predicting Social Behavior*, Englewood Cliffs, N.J.: Prentice-Hall, 1980.

American Association for the Advancement of Science, *Benchmarks for Science Literacy*, New York: Oxford University Press, 1993.

Anderson, L. W., "Curricular Alignment: A Re-Examination," *Theory into Practice*, Vol. 41, No. 4, 2002, pp. 25–60.

Benjamini, Y., and Y. Hochberg, "Controlling the False Discovery Rate: A Practical and Powerful Approach to Multiple Testing," *Journal of the Royal Statistical Society*, Series B, Vol. 57, 1995, pp. 289–300.

Borman, K., and G. Kersaint, *Assessing the Impact of the National Science Foundation's Urban Systemic Initiative*, Sarasota, Fla.: University of South Florida, David C. Anchin Center, 2002.

Boyd, S. E., E. R. Banilower, J. D. Pasley, and I. R. Weiss, *Progress and Pitfalls: A Cross-Site Look at Local Systemic Change Through Teacher Enhancement*, Chapel Hill, N.C.: Horizon Research, Inc., 2003. Available at http://www.horizon-research.com/LSC/news/progress_and_pitfalls. pdf; last accessed May 31, 2006.

Burstein, L., L. McDonnell, J. Van Winkle, T. Ormseth, J. Mirocha, and G. Guiton, *Validating National Curriculum Indicators*, Santa Monica, Calif.: RAND Corporation, MR-658-NSF, 1995.

Camburn, E., and C. Barnes, "Assessing the Validity of a Language Arts Instruction Log Through Triangulation," *Elementary School Journal*, Vol. 105, 2004, pp. 49–74.

Chau, D., V. Williams, V. Le, A. Robyn, B. Stecher, and L. Hamilton, "Teachers as Implementers of Mathematics and Science Systemic Reform Policies," Santa Monica, Calif.: RAND Corporation, WR-338-NSF, 2006.

Cimbricz, S., "State-Mandated Testing and Teachers' Beliefs and Practice," *Education Policy Analysis Archives*, Vol. 10, No. 2, 2002.

Cohen, D. K., "A Revolution in One Classroom: The Case of Mrs. Oublier," *Educational Evaluation and Policy Analysis*, Vol. 14, 1990, pp. 327–345.

Cohen, D. K., and H. C. Hill, "Instructional Policy and Classroom Performance: The Mathematics Reform in California," *Teachers College Record*, Vol. 102, No. 2, 2000, pp. 294–343.

Committee on Science, Engineering, and Public Policy, *Rising Above the Gathering Storm: Energizing and Employing America for a Brighter Economic Future*, Washington, D.C.: National Academies Press, 2006. Available at http://www.nap.edu/books/0309100399/html; last accessed May 5, 2006.

Corcoran, T. B., P. M. Shields, and A. A. Zucker, *Evaluations of the National Science Foundation's Statewide Systemic Initiatives (SSI) Program: The SSI's and Professional Development for Teachers*, Menlo Park, Calif.: SRI International, 1998.

Desimone, L. M., and K. C. Le Floch, "Are We Asking the Right Questions? Using Cognitive Interviews to Improve Surveys in Education Research," *Educational Evaluation and Policy Analysis*, Vol. 26, No. 1, 2004, pp. 1–22.

Desimone, L. M., T. M. Smith, K. Ueno, and D. P. Baker, "The Distribution of Teaching Quality in Mathematics: Assessing Barriers to the Reform of United States Mathematics Instruction from an International Perspective," *American Educational Research Journal*, Vol. 42, No. 3, 2005, pp. 501–535.

Dutro, E., M. C. Fisk, R. Koch, L. J. Roop, and K. Wixson, "When State Policies Meet Local District Contexts: Standards-Based Professional Development as a Means to Individual Agency and Collective Ownership," *Teachers College Record*, Vol. 104, No. 4, 2002, pp. 787–811.

Ferguson, R. F., and H. F. Ladd, "How and Why Money Matters: An Analysis of Alabama Schools," in H. F. Ladd, ed., *Holding Schools Accountable: Performance-Based Reform in Education*, Washington, D.C.: Brookings Institution Press, 1996, pp. 265–298.

Gamoran, A., "Schooling and Achievement: Additive Versus Interactive Models," in S. W. Raudenbush and J. D. Willms, eds., *Schools, Classrooms, and Pupils: International Studies of Schooling from a Multilevel Perspective*, San Diego, Calif.: Academic Press, 1991, pp. 37–51.

Gamoran, A., A. C. Porter, J. Smithson, and P. A. White, "Upgrading High School Mathematics Instruction: Improving Learning Opportunities for Low-Achieving, Low-Income Youth," *Educational Evaluation and Policy Analysis*, Vol. 19, 1997, pp. 325–338.

Gelman, A. B., J. S. Carlin, H. S. Stern, and D. B. Rubin, *Bayesian Data Analysis*, London: Chapman & Hall, 1995.

Goertz, M. E., "Invited Commentary: Educational Reform and Instructional Change," *Education Statistics Quarterly*, Vol. 1, No. 2, 1999, pp. 14–16.

Goldhaber, D. D., and D. J. Brewer, "Does Teacher Certification Matter? High School Teacher Certification Status and Student Achievement," *Educational Evaluation and Policy Analysis*, Vol. 22, No. 2, 2000, pp. 129–145.

Hamilton, L. S., D. F. McCaffrey, B. M. Stecher, S. P. Klein, S. P., A. Robyn, and D. Bugliari, "Studying Large-Scale Reforms of Instructional Practice: An Example from Mathematics and Science," *Educational Evaluation and Policy Analysis*, Vol. 25, No. 1, 2003, pp. 1–29.

Harcourt Assessment (formerly Harcourt Brace Educational Measurement), *Stanford Achievement Test: Open-Ended Scoring Guide—Science*, Chicago, 1996a.

———, *Stanford Achievement Test: Open-Ended Scoring Guide—Mathematics*, Chicago, 1996b.

Henke, R. R., X. Chen, and G. Goldman, *What Happens in Classrooms? Instructional Practices in Elementary and Secondary Schools: 1994–1995*, Washington, D.C.: U.S. Department of Education, NCES 1999-348, 1999.

Herman, J., D. Klein, and J. Abedi, "Assessing Student's Opportunity to Learn: Teacher and Student Perspectives," *Educational Measurement: Issues and Practice*, Vol. 19, No. 4, 2000, pp. 16–24.

Hill, H. C., "Content Across Communities: Validating Measures of Elementary Mathematics Instruction," *Educational Policy*, Vol. 19, No. 3, 2005, pp. 447–475.

Hoachlander, G., J. Griffith, and J. Ralph, *From Data to Information: New Directions for the National Center for Education Statistics*, Washington, D.C.: U.S. Department of Education, NCES 96-901, 1996.

Ihaka, R., and R. Gentleman, "A Language for Data Analysis and Graphics," *Journal of Computational and Graphical Statistics*, Vol. 5, 1996, pp. 299–314.

Ingle, M., and S. Cory, "Classroom Implementation of the National Science Education Standards: A Snapshot Instrument to Provide Feedback and Reflection for Teachers," *Science Educator*, Vol. 8, 1999, pp. 49–54.

Kennedy, M. M., "Approximations to Indicators of Student Outcomes," *Educational Evaluation and Policy Analysis*, Vol. 21, No. 4, 1999, pp. 345–363.

Klein, S., L. Hamilton, D. McCaffrey, B. Stecher, A. Robyn, and D. Burroughs, *Teaching Practices and Student Achievement: Report of First-Year Findings from the "Mosaic" Study of Systemic Initiatives in Mathematics and Science*, Santa Monica, Calif.: RAND Corporation, MR-1233-EDU, 2000.

Landis, J., and G. G. Koch, "The Measurement of Observer Agreement for Categorical Data," *Biometrics*, Vol. 33, 1977, pp. 159–174.

Le, V., K. Kerr, A. Robyn, B. Stecher, and L. Hamilton, "An Examination of the Validity of Teachers' Responses to Vignette-Based Measures of Reform Instruction," paper presented at the annual meeting of the American Educational Research Association, San Francisco, 2006.

Linn, M. C., C. Kessel, K. Lee, J. Levenson, M. Spitulnik, and J. D. Slotta, "Teaching and Learning K–8 Mathematics and Science Through Inquiry: Program Reviews and Recommendations," unpublished report commissioned by the North Central Regional Educational Laboratory, 2000. Available at http://www.ncrel.org/engauge/resource/techno/k8.htm; last accessed May 31, 2006.

Lockwood J. R., H. Doran, and D. F. McCaffrey, "Using R for Estimating Longitudinal Student Achievement Models," *The R Newsletter*, Vol. 3, No. 3, 2003, pp. 17–23.

Lockwood, J. R., D. F. McCaffrey, L. T. Mariano, and C. Setodji, "Bayesian Methods for Scalable Multi-Subject Value-Added Assessment," *Journal of Educational and Behavioral Statistics*, in press.

Ma, L., *Knowing and Teaching Elementary Mathematics: Teachers' Understanding of Fundamental Mathematics in China and the United States*, Mahwah, N.J.: Lawrence Erlbaum Associates, 1999.

Martinez-Fernandez, J. F., *A Multilevel Study of the Effects of Opportunity to Learn (OTL) on Student Reading Achievement: Issues of Measurement, Equity, and Validity*, unpublished doctoral dissertation, University of California, Los Angeles, 2005.

Mayer, D. P., "Do New Teaching Standards Undermine Performance on Old Tests?" *Educational Evaluation and Policy Analysis*, Vol. 20, 1998, pp. 53–73.

———, "Measuring Instructional Practice: Can Policymakers Trust Survey Data?" *Educational Evaluation and Policy Analysis*, Vol. 21, 1999, pp. 29–45.

McCaffrey D. F., J. R. Lockwood, D. Koretz, T. A. Louis, and L. Hamilton, "Models for Value-Added Modeling of Teacher Effects," *Journal of Educational and Behavioral Statistics*, Vol. 29, No. 1, 2004, pp. 67–101.

McLaughlin, M. W., and J. E. Talbert, *Contexts That Matter for Teaching and Learning: Strategic Opportunities for Meeting the Nation's Education Goals*, Stanford, Calif.: Stanford University, Center for Research on the Context of Secondary School Teaching, 1993.

Mullis, I. V. S., M. O. Martin, E. J. Gonzalez, and S. J. Chrostowski, *Findings from IEA's Trends in International Mathematics and Science Study at the Fourth and Eighth Grades*, Chestnut Hill, Mass.: Boston College, TIMSS and PIRLS International Study Center, 2004.

Muthen, B., L. Huang, B. Jo, S. Khoo, G. N. Goff, J. Novak, and J. Shih, *Opportunity-to-Learn Effects on Achievement: Analytical Aspects*, Los Angeles: University of California, National Center for Research on Evaluation, Standards, and Student Testing, 1995.

National Council of Teachers of Mathematics (NCTM), *Curriculum and Evaluation Standards for School Mathematics*, Reston, Va., 1989.

———, *Principles and Standards for School Mathematics*, Reston, Va., 2000.

National Research Council (NRC), *National Science Standards*, Washington, D.C.: National Academy Press, 1996.

Pedulla, J. J., L. M. Abrams, G. F. Madaus, M. K. Russell, M. A. Ramos, and M. Jing, *Perceived Effects of State-Mandated Testing Programs on Teaching and Learning: Findings from a National Survey of Teachers*, Boston: Boston College, Lynch School of Education, 2003.

Pinheiro, J., and D. M. Bates, *Mixed-Effects Models in S and S-PLUS*, New York: Springer, 2000.

Porter, A. C., M. W. Kirst, E. Osthoff, J. L. Smithson, and S. A. Schneider, *Reform of High School Mathematics and Science and Opportunity to Learn*, New Brunswick, N.J.: Rutgers University, Consortium for Policy Research in Education, 1994.

Raudenbush, S. W., and A. S. Bryk, *Hierarchical Linear Models: Applications and Data Analysis Methods*, Newbury Park, Calif.: Sage Publications, 2002.

Ravitz, J. L., H. J. Becker, and Y. T. Wong, *Constructivist-Compatible Beliefs and Practices Among U.S. Teachers*, Irvine, Calif.: Center for Research on Information Technology and Organizations, 2000.

Rowan, B., E. Camburn, and R. Correnti, "Using Teacher Logs to Measure the Enacted Curriculum in Large-Scale Surveys: A Study of Literacy Teaching in 3rd Grade Classrooms," *Elementary School Journal*, Vol. 105, 2004, pp. 75–102.

Rowan, B., R. Correnti, and R. J. Miller, "What Large-Scale Survey Research Tells Us About Teacher Effects on Student Achievement: Insights from the Prospects Study of Elementary Schools," *The Teachers College Record*, Vol. 104, No. 8, 2002, pp. 1525–1567.

Rowan, B., D. Harrison, and A. Hayes, "Using Instructional Logs to Study Elementary School Mathematics: A Close Look at Curriculum and Teaching in the Early Grades," *Elementary School Journal*, Vol. 105, 2004, pp. 103–127.

Ruiz-Primo, M. A., and M. Li, "Vignettes as an Alternative Teacher Evaluation Instrument: An Exploratory Study," paper presented at the annual meeting of the American Educational Research Association, New Orleans, La., 2002.

Russon, C., L. Stark, and J. Horn, *Rural Systemic Initiative Survey*, Kalamazoo, Mich.: Western Michigan University, The Evaluation Center, 2000.

Sanders, W. L., A. M. Saxton, and B. P. Horn, "The Tennessee Value-Added Assessment System: A Quantitative Outcomes-Based Approach to Educational Assessment," in J. Millman, ed., *Grading Teachers, Grading Schools: Is Student Achievement a Valid Evaluational Measure?* Thousand Oaks, Calif.: Corwin Press, Inc., 1997, pp. 137–162.

Saxe, G. B., M. Gearhart, and M. Seltzer, "Relations Between Classroom Practices and Student Learning in the Domain of Fractions," *Cognition and Instruction*, Vol. 17, No. 1, 1999, pp. 1–24.

Schafer, J. L., *Analysis of Incomplete Multivariate Data*, New York: Chapman & Hall, 1997.

Schmidt, W. H., and C. C. McKnight, "Surveying Educational Opportunity in Mathematics and Science: An International Perspective," *Educational Evaluation and Policy Analysis*, Vol. 17, 1995, pp. 337–353.

Schoenfeld, A. H., "Teaching Mathematical Thinking and Problem Solving," in L. B. Resnick and L. E. Klopfer, eds., *Toward the Thinking Curriculum: Current Cognitive Research/Association for Supervision and Curriculum Development Yearbook*, Washington, D.C.: Association for Supervision and Curriculum Development, 1989, pp. 83–103.

Shields, P., T. Corcoran, and A. Zucker, *Evaluation of NSF's Statewide Systemic Initiatives (SSI) Program: First-Year Report, Volume I: Technical Report*, Menlo Park, Calif.: SRI International, 1994.

Shields, P. M., J. A. Marsh, and N. E. Adelman, *Evaluation of the National Science Foundation's Statewide Systemic Initiatives (SSI) Program: The SSI's Impacts on Classroom Practice*, Menlo Park, Calif.: SRI International, 1998.

Smerdon, B. A., D. T. Burkam, and V. E. Lee, "Access to Constructivist and Didactic Teaching: Who Gets It? Where Is It Practiced?" *Teachers College Record*, Vol. 101, 1999, pp. 5–34.

Smith, J., V. Lee, and F. Newmann, *Instruction and Achievement in Chicago Elementary Schools: Improving Chicago's Schools*, Chicago: Consortium on Chicago School Research, 2001.

Smith, M. S., and J. O'Day, "Systemic School Reform," in S. H. Fuhrman and B. Malen, eds., *The Politics of Curriculum and Testing*, Bristol, Pa.: Falmer Press, 1991, pp. 233–268.

Spiegelhalter, D. J., A. Thomas, and N. G. Best, *WinBUGS: Bayesian Inference Using Gibbs Sampling*, Cambridge, United Kingdom: MRC Biostatistics Unit, 1999.

Spillane, J. P., and J. S. Zeuli, "Reform and Teaching: Exploring Patterns of Practice in the Context of National and State Mathematics Reforms," *Educational Evaluation and Policy Analysis*, Vol. 21, No. 1, 1999, pp. 1–28.

Stecher, B. M., and S. P. Klein, eds., *Performance Assessments in Science: Hands-On Tasks and Scoring Guide*, Santa Monica, Calif.: RAND Corporation, MR-660-NSF, 1996.

Stecher, B., V. Le, L. Hamilton, G. Ryan, A. Robyn, and J. R. Lockwood, "Using Structured Classroom Vignettes to Measure Instructional Practices in Mathematics," *Educational Evaluation and Policy Analysis*, Vol. 28, No. 2, 2006, pp. 101–129.

Stigler, J. W., and M. Perry, "Developing Classroom Process Data for the Improvement of Teaching," in N. S. Raju, J. W. Pellegrino, M. W. Bertenthal, K. J. Mitchell, and L. R. Jones, eds., *Grading the Nation's Report Card: Research from the Evaluation of NAEP*, Washington, D.C.: National Academy Press, 2000, pp. 229–264.

Supovitz, J. A., D. P. Mayer, and J. B. Kahle, "Promoting Inquiry-Based Instructional Practice: The Longitudinal Impact of Professional Development in the Context of Systemic Reform," *Educational Policy*, Vol. 14, No. 3, 2000, pp. 331–356.

Swanson, C. B., and D. L. Stevenson, "Standards-Based Reform in Practice: Evidence on State Policy and Classroom Instruction from the NAEP State Assessments," *Educational Evaluation and Policy Analysis*, Vol. 24, No. 1, 2002, pp. 1–27.

Thompson, D., and S. Senk, "The Effects of Curriculum on Achievement in Second Year Algebra: The Example of the University of Chicago Mathematics Project," *Journal for Research in Mathematics Education*, Vol. 32, No. 1, 2001, pp. 58–84.

U.S. Department of Education, National Center for Education Statistics [National Educational Longitudinal Study of 1988 Second Follow-Up], *Constructed Response Tests in the NELS:88 High School Effectiveness Study*, Washington, D.C., NCES 97-804, 1997 (authored by J. M. Pollock and D. A. Rock; project officer: P. Quinn).

Venables, W. N., D. M. Smith, and the R Development Core Team, *An Introduction to R, Notes on R: A Programming Environment for Data Analysis and Graphics*, 2005. Available at http://cran.r-project.org/doc/manuals/R-intro.pdf; last accessed May 31, 2006.

Von Secker, C. E., and R. W. Lissitz, "Estimating the Impact of Instructional Practices on Student Achievement in Science," *Journal of Research in Science Teaching*, Vol. 36, No. 10, 1999, pp. 1110–1126.

Webb, N. L., *Criteria for Alignment of Expectations and Assessments in Mathematics and Science Education*, Madison, Wisc.: University of Wisconsin–Madison, National Institute for Science Education, Research Monograph No. 6, 1997.

Wenglinsky, H., "How Schools Matter: The Link Between Teacher Classroom Practices and Student Academic Performance," *Education Policy Analysis Archives*, Vol. 10, No. 12, 2002. Available at http://epaa.asu.edu/epaa/v10n12/; last accessed May 5, 2006.

Williams, L., *The Urban Systemic Initiatives Program of the National Science Foundation: Summary Update*, Arlington, Va.: National Science Foundation, 1998.

Yoon, B., and L. B. Resnick, *Instructional Validity, Opportunity to Learn and Equity: New Standards Examinations for the California Mathematics Renaissance*, Los Angeles: University of California, National Center for Research on Evaluation, Standards, and Student Testing, CSE Technical Report 484, 1998.